The Road to Effective Reading

Proceedings of the tenth annual study conference of
the United Kingdom Reading Association,
Totley-Thornbridge 1973

Editor William Latham

Ward Lock Educational

ISBN 0 7062 3407 3 paperback
     0 7062 3406 5 hardbound

First published 1975

Set in 10 on 11 point Press Roman, IBM
by Trade Linotype Limited, Birmingham
for Ward Lock Educational
116 Baker Street, London W1M 2BB
Made in England

Contents

Introduction

The tenth annual study conference of the United Kingdom Reading Association, held at Totley-Thornbridge College of Education, Sheffield, was dedicated to the proposition that learning to read, properly considered, is a long-term developmental process, beginning in preschool life and language experience and reaching fruition in the study skills of the effective adult reader. The range of papers presented at the Conference does much to support this proposition.

It seems probable that the publication of these proceedings will be linked in time with the appearance of the Bullock Committee's report. The nature of that report is as yet unknown, but it may well be that it will recommend changes in aims, method, organization and assessment procedures in the teaching of reading. If this is so, debate must come before action if anything lasting is to be achieved. The papers in these proceedings are a contribution to such debate.

William Latham

Day 1
Convenor: Derek Thackray

1 The teaching of reading – a crisis?

William Latham

Introduction

In 1972 a committee, now known as the Bullock Committee, was brought into being by the Government to consider, in relation to schools, all aspects of teaching the use of English, including reading, writing and speech; how present practice might be improved; the role that initial and in-service training might play; and to what extent the arrangements for monitoring the general level of attainment in these skills could be introduced or improved.

The setting up of the Committee followed hard upon the heels of the report of a survey, carried out by the NFER, involving pupils in the last year of primary education, and those in the last compulsory year of secondary education (Start and Wells 1972). Two tests of literal comprehension, both multiple choice, were used. The results obtained suggested that, at best, there had been no improvement in standards of reading comprehension, as measured by the tests, since the early 1960s, and indicated the possibility that the standard of the younger group had even fallen since 1964.

These results need to be treated with a degree of caution for several reasons: some schools declined to take part; there was a high degree of absenteeism in the secondary group on the relevant day; and some of the words (e.g. mannequin, haberdasher) used in the tests were outdated.

But other surveys have also produced results suggestive of difficulties in the early stages of learning to read.

Gardner reported that, in 1961, 25 per cent of a sample of 2,000 first year juniors had not made a start in learning to read; the figure had risen to 40 per cent by 1967 (Gardner 1968).

Davie, Butler and Goldstein (1972), reporting on the National Child Development study of 1965, covering 11,000 children in their last term in the infant school, commented that:

> . . . the most striking feature to emerge from the results is that the proportion of good readers in Scotland is markedly higher than any other region of Britain. This difference is even more marked for poor readers . . . for every eighteen poor readers in Scotland there were proportionately twenty-nine poor readers in England, and thirty in Wales.

A survey carried out by the Inner London Education Authority, involving 31,000 eight year olds produced the fact that 17 per cent were at least two years retarded in reading (ILEA 1969).

It seems, therefore, that despite doubts concerning the reliability of data from surveys, it is not unreasonable to assume that standards in certain aspects of learning to read have not risen over the last decade, and that the possibility exists that they have fallen.

But is, or should, our aim be limited to improving the performance of our pupils in word recognition or multiple-choice literal comprehension tests? In my view it should not. Our aim should be to play our part in helping our pupils to become effective adult readers, with a positive attitude to reading as a source of profit and pleasure.

The effective reader

What are the attributes of the effective reader? It can be plausibly argued that, in the area of study, he possesses skills relevant to finding, understanding and retaining information for future use. He is also able, by adjusting speed of reading to material and purpose, to reduce the time required to obtain information to a personal minimum.

One would expect to find a large number of effective readers amongst our undergraduate population since their need for the relevant skills is obviously great; and it is not unreasonable to assume that they would have been the higher achievers in reading surveys of the type described above. This expectation, however, does not appear to be fulfilled.

For example, in a report of a committee set up by the University Grants Committee (UGC 1967) considerable doubt is thrown on the ability of many university students even to find the books and articles they require. In one survey in the report, involving some 1,300 students, it was said that 'the proportion of students who claimed to know of the existence of bibliographical tools in their libraries was as follows: abstracts 37 per cent; indexes 33 per cent.' Further, only 13 per cent reported that they had been taught to use such tools, and even when dealing with subject and author catalogues, '28 per cent and 22 per cent respectively of the students interviewed did not know whether their main university libraries had subject and author catalogues.' It is a little worrying to note that 75 per cent of the students interviewed had used their secondary school libraries, but only 40 per cent reported that they had been trained how to do so.

More recently Mann (1973), writing of a survey carried out at Sheffield University reports that, 16 per cent of the students involved said that they did not use a library; and 35 per cent of the total did not have a book from the university library at the time of the survey. One of his main conclusions was that 'undergraduates, on the whole, are uninstructed about the use of books'. It would seem, indeed, that some students avoid problems concerning lack of knowledge of library organization and how to use books by not using the library!

Even, however, if books are sought and found are they used efficiently? In 1967, when I was on the staff of the London Institute of Education, I sent a very open-ended questionnaire to ninety university lecturers teaching medical and dental students, and students reading for degrees in the social and physical sciences, asking for information concerning the level of literacy of their students. Fifty-two lecturers replied, and were virtually unanimous in reporting their students as 'illiterate'. One lecturer did, however, say that the best of his students overcame this handicap by the end of the course! In the area of the use of books the students were considered 'slow readers', 'unable to select the essential from the unessential', or to make 'usable notes' from their reading.

In view of such studies it is not unreasonable to suggest that we are not succeeding to the degree that we would wish in our task of helping our pupils to become effective readers—and this is no small matter when we considered 'slow readers', 'unable to select the essential from the inessential', or to make 'usable notes' from their reading.

Can we, however, consider that we have reached a crisis in the teaching of reading? My answer would be 'Yes', because the problems that we face in the successful teaching of reading, and which given time we might overcome, are only half the story.

The other half of the story

The other half of the story concerns a growing criticism of state education and, more particularly, of the 'child-centred' approaches to teaching which the primary school fosters.

This criticism covers a whole spectrum of attitudes; from a reasoned appeal for more structure in the curriculum (including more direct teaching), and more effective ways of monitoring the progress of the individual child so that we can be sure that necessary knowledge and skills are being acquired; through a plea for a return to the elitism, formal teaching, and strict discipline which it is claimed characterized our work in a mythical golden age of education; to, finally, a yearning, of doubtful psychological origin, for those panaceas for all our educational and social ills, the cane, the birch, and the rope!

That the 'golden age' movement has influential supporters is not in doubt. The so-called *Black Papers* of 1969-70 (Cox and Dyson 1971) make this clear, and there may well be something in the claim, made in the introduction to *Black Paper Three* (Cox and Dyson 1970) that the first Black Paper 'was greeted with enthusiasm by thousands of experienced teachers'. It is not unreasonable for teachers, punch-drunk with innovation in methods, organization (and, in reading, even medium), by no means supported by acceptable evidence concerning possible value, to yearn for a 'golden age' when they knew what they had to teach and how to teach it, and were, on the whole, left to get on with it. This is particularly likely when there is insufficient in-service training to help them sort the gold from the dross, and learn to use effectively what may be of value; and when they are faced with overlarge classes and, often, inadequate working conditions.

In the Black Papers present standards of literacy come under attack.

For example, Sir Cyril Burt, an educationist with an international reputation, claims that present standards in reading 'judged by tests applied and standardized in 1913-14, average standards in reading . . . are now appreciably lower than they were fifty-five years ago' (Burt 1969); whilst Cox and Dyson claim that 'the sad truth is that still today hundreds of students whose standards in English are very low are being sent out as qualified teachers' (Cox and Dyson 1971).

The blame for the suggested failure to obtain acceptable standards in basic skills is placed squarely on the primary schools with attacks on 'the modern craze for child-centred education' (Gardner 1968); 'so-called learning from experience' (Barzun 1970); progressive methods 'not suited to the average teacher' (Cox and Dyson 1969); and a claim that because of such methods 'it is possible for an intelligent child to spend three years in an infant school and emerge with a sight vocabulary of twenty words and no word skills' (Green 1969).

Thus, it can be claimed that a crisis associated with the teaching of reading does exist. For not only do we face difficulties in our task of producing effective readers, but our difficulties are contributing to a backlash which could lead not to a rational examination of our problems, but to an attempt to turn back the clock and revive the authoritarianism and learning without understanding which characterized what was worst in our educational system in an earlier age.

What are our needs?

If one accepts that a crisis exists, then it is necessary to consider what needs to be done to meet it. In my view we need to:

1   redefine the nature of our task—to say clearly what we mean when we say that someone can read. For the way we define the nature of the task will influence our aims and, through them the outcome of our work.
2   develop a more systematic approach to teaching and the recording of individual progress.
3   give serious consideration to the choosing of areas for research, and the means by which we communicate our results to our colleagues in schools.
4   give priority to a demand for an increase in the provision of in-service training, and for a close examination of the means by which such training can be most effectively given.

The nature of the task

If we continue to define reading in terms of decoding (e.g. the ability to turn the written into the spoken word) we shall find ourselves in agreement with the Plowden Committee when it states that 'traditionally one of the first tasks of the infant school was to teach the child to read. It is still quite rightly a major preoccupation' (DES 1967). So agreeing we shall continue to fail the student teacher and the teacher and child in the school.

One result of an acceptance of the definition given above will be that training in teaching for the early stages of learning to read will be restricted to students preparing to teach in first or infant schools. This, despite evidence that suggests that more than 40 per cent of the children entering the junior school require help associated with the beginnings of learning to read (Morris 1959, Kellmer Pringle *et al* 1966). It is worthy of note that an ILEA survey found that 63 per cent of all their junior schools or departments had no full-time teacher who had 'received specific/detailed training ... to teach reading' (ILEA 1969).

A further result will be that no attempt will be made to train students destined for primary or secondary school how to bridge the gap between the beginnings of reading and the skills of the adult reader, and consequently these skills will not be acquired.

In the schools, as a result of our faulty conceptualization of reading, readiness for beginning reading will continue to be based on the child's age (and, thus, his position within the educational system) rather than his readiness for the task. For many children this will lead to frustration and failure and, consequently, to a negative attitude to subject, school and teachers.

The teacher in the first or infant school may well become frustrated and unhappy. On the one hand, many of her pupils will fail to reach the goals she has set for them; on the other, she will be aware of the scarcity of colleagues in the junior or middle school able to help children in the early stages of learning to read.

Furthermore, teachers in secondary schools, colleges and universities, unaware of the need or the methods required to bridge the gap between the beginnings of reading and the higher order reading skills, will become increasingly worried or angry because their students are not effective readers.

If, however, we define reading in terms of the attributes of the effective adult reader rather than in terms of its beginnings, then a new pattern of teacher training and teaching in schools may well emerge.

First, there could be a moving away from the assumption that reading is something which a child is taught at some specific point in the school system and, thus, the beginnings of reading are more likely to be related to the child's readiness in terms of sensory, intellectual, social and emotional development, and life and language experience rather than to its place in infant or first school. Further, once readiness for reading is seen in developmental terms, it is only a small step to an appreciation of the relationship of reading to listening, speaking, and writing. Second, it is highly probable that we would see the development of a reading curriculum which would take children from the beginnings of reading to adult reading skills.

Such changes would lead to many more of our pupils becoming effective readers, and fewer suffering failure, with a consequent reduction in the level of teacher frustration. Furthermore, a realization and an acceptance of the relationship between preschool life and language experience and success in the early stages of learning to read might well produce a better relationship between teacher and parent, for it might lead to a stress on the complementary rather than competitive nature of their respective roles.

In the colleges one would expect changes aimed at giving students undergoing initial training an overview of the teaching of reading and expertise in depth in that area of the curriculum in which they would be mainly involved. This should logically lead to ensuring that students destined for middle or junior schools have an expertise related to the beginnings of reading, and a working knowledge of the study skill levels normally associated with the secondary schools.

Further, it would lead to the development of in-service courses, such as the Diploma in the Teaching of Reading at Totley-Thornbridge, which would produce specialists able to help and advise at any level of the reading curriculum.

Concerning the employment of reading specialists, I feel strongly that the use of teacher-advisers, who would be qualified teachers with a specialist qualification in the teaching of reading, working side by side with teachers, in schools, as well as teachers centres, would provide a new and effective approach to in- service training. This is not to decry the good work of present local advisers, but to argue that there is room for peripatetic helpers, unburdened by administrative tasks, who would be able to spend all their time working with teachers. Promotion to a post as adviser, with all the activities outside the schools that this normally implies, might then well be made from the ranks of the teacher-advisers.

Summary
In summary, I would argue that a redefinition of the term 'reading' would lead to more effective initial and in-service training; more effective readers; fewer failures in the early stages of learning to read; fewer frustrated teachers—and finally less ammunition for those who mount irrational attacks on primary education.

It may be argued that the definition of reading which I am advocating is accepted widely enough for my plea to be out of date, however relevant it may have been when I first made it at an international conference in 1966 (Latham 1967). I am, however, reasonably certain, on the basis of my own and my students' experiences, that the implications of such acceptance have not progressed beyond some academic writers, a few colleges of education, and a limited number of schools.

A systematic approach to teaching and the recording of progress
If we consider that success in our task as teachers demands that we concern ourselves with the establishment of clear relevant aims, efficient actions and valid assessment procedures, then further needs arise.

First, we must associate ourselves with efforts in schools, teachers centres or colleges, to establish a reading curriculum stretching from beginning skills to adult skills. Second, we must be clear about our objectives for the child in relation to his needs, attainments and ability, and how much direct teaching has to occur if these objectives are to be reached. Finally, we must record the progress of the individual in such a way that the teacher, whether the class may be new to her or not, can plan effectively for further individual progress, or identify the child whose progress is being impeded by lack of knowledge or skills.

We shall serve the child and society ill if we do not relate the child's needs and abilities to a reading curriculum in which structure is optimal, and assessment procedures chart the pupil's progress towards identifiable objectives. Without these factors few children will become effective adult readers.

Research
Here our needs are to relate our research to the felt needs of the teacher, and the realities of the classroom; to coordinate effort as far as may be possible; and to communicate successfully the results, and their implications, to colleagues in school and colleges.

If we are to relate our research to teacher needs, we must obtain information directly from teachers concerning problems and priorities. The result of the recent survey undertaken by the Research Subcommittee of the UKRA among practising teachers offers some useful leads. These results have been forwarded to the Bullock Committee as part of the Association's evidence to that body and one would hope that the Committee's report will contain some reference to them.

Concerning coordination of effort, in an ideal world all those planning research would know what has already taken place and what is planned by others for the future. At the present time the information available is inadequate, and we should, therefore, give our support to any promising attempt to make good this situation.

Successful communication requires a partnership between teacher and researcher—perhaps, ideally, they should be the same person! The success of such a partnership would depend, to a marked degree, on the researcher's knowledge of teaching and the teacher's needs, and on the teacher's acceptance of the methods of research—the acceptance being based on an understanding of the value of such methods, and their limitations.

To achieve a successful partnership will not be easy. I would suggest, very tentatively, that we might move towards it if:

1   colleges of education encourage their students to try, from the beginning of their courses, to consider critically all they see, read or hear.
2   in initial and in-service training provision is made for acquiring knowledge and experience of the methods of educational research.
3   the researcher sees the teacher as a partner in the enterprise (and shows that he does!), rather than a convenient device for gathering data.
4   educationists with training and experience in research are prepared to help groups of teachers to set up their own projects and interpret their results.

Better teaching requires greater knowledge. If we can coordinate research into relevant problems, and communicate our results to colleagues who can understand and use them, that knowledge will become available.

In-service training

That we need in-service training is not in doubt for, as Sir Ronald Gould observed, 'no teacher can afford to spend a lifetime relying on the capital he has acquired in the years of initial training' (Schools Council 1970). The more so, one might add, in an era of challenge and change. If the hopes raised by the James Committee are realized, teachers will have in-service training as a right. But do we yet know the optimal form of such training? In what respect, and for what purpose, are workshops better than lectures? Would weekend courses be a good idea? What about summer schools? Is the one-term course an acceptable substitute for present full year courses? What should be the roles of reading centres and teachers centres in in-service training? What should be the role of the college of education in such training? What combination of methods of presentation and duration of course would best serve the needs of teachers in an area (including those left behind in schools when others are on courses)?

These, I think, are some of the questions to which we need to find a tentative answer in the months to come, for effective in-service training may well be an important factor in deciding the future of primary education.

Conclusion

In conclusion I would like to say that I consider that a sense of urgency and mission is required if our pupils are to follow the road to effective reading, with all that that implies; and if, at the same time, we are to preserve what is best in primary education from the effects of premature judgment and ill-considered action.

References

BARZUN, J. (1970) 'The centrality of reading' in C. B. Cox and A. E. Dyson (Eds) *Black Paper Three: Goodbye Mr Short* London: The Critical Quarterly Society

BURT, C. (1969) 'The mental differences between children' in C. B. Cox and A. E. Dyson (Eds) *Black Paper Two: The Crisis in Education* London: The Critical Quarterly Society

COX, C. and DYSON, A. E. (Eds) (1969) *Black Paper Two: The Crisis in Education* London: The Critical Quarterly Society

COX, C. and DYSON, A. E. (Eds) (1971) *The Black Papers on Education* London: Davis-Poynter

COX, C. and DYSON, A. E. (Eds) (1970) *Black Paper Three: Goodbye Mr Short* London: The Critical Quarterly Society

DAVIE, R. *et al* (1972) *From Birth to Seven* London: Longman

DES (1967) *Children and their Primary Schools Volume I* (Plowden Report) London: HMSO

GARDNER, K. (1968) in N. Smart (Ed) *Crisis in the Classroom* London: IPC

GREEN, N. W. (1969) An American lesson in beginning reading *Reading* 3, 2 quoted in C. B. Cox and A. E. Dyson (Eds) *Black Paper Two: The Crisis in Education* London: The Critical Quarterly Society

KELLMER PRINGLE, M. L. *et al* (1966) *11,000 Seven Year Olds* London: Longman

ILEA (1969) *Literacy Survey* London: ILEA

LATHAM, W. (1968) 'Are today's teachers adequately trained in the teaching of reading?' in J. Downing and A. L. Brown (Eds) *Third International Reading Symposium* London: Cassell

MANN, P. (1973) *Books and Students* London: National Book League

MORRIS, J. (1959) *Reading in the Primary School* Slough: NFER

START, K. B. and WELLS, B. K. (1972) *The Trend of Reading Standards* Slough: NFER

UNIVERSITY GRANTS COMMITTEE (1967) *Report of the Committee on Libraries* London: HMSO

2 Language and reading—a study of early reading

Margaret Clark

Introduction

A great deal of attention has been directed to the deficits which the child brings to the initial reading task, to the lack of stimulation in many homes and indeed to the general unreadiness of many children for the school situation. Reading readiness studies have, however, contributed little to the more effective teaching of reading. If one approaches the teaching of reading from an analysis of the skills and knowledge the child has already acquired when he begins learning to read, and the additional knowledge and skills required for fluent reading, one may be led to the conclusion that the present approaches to the initial teaching of reading miss some of the crucial features required for the development of such a skill. Too much emphasis may be placed on training skills such as precise visual scanning of letters or words; while the important features may be *discrimination* and *anticipation* within a language context, rather than identification. A distinction must be made between the language awareness required in order to learn to appreciate the significant characteristics of print, and the understanding of the subtleties of language required in order to make progress when subjected to the complicated, and often imprecise, terminology in some early reading instruction. It seems important that attention should be directed to language and the extent to which that is a crucial variable in the development of successful reading, not only the oral language interaction between child and adult but also the specific language of the reading instruction and the language of the books used in the early stages.

A greater insight into how to teach reading will not come automatically from an appreciation of the variables which are crucial in the development of oral language competence. It is nevertheless important to analyse some of the pitfalls into which oral language programmes have fallen and consider whether these have significance for the understanding of written language. The assumptions that deprived children are deficient either in quantity of vocabulary or in awareness of a range of grammatic structures, both assumptions leading to specific types of language programmes, have been shown to be fallacious. Again, the idea that deprived children would improve if 'bombarded with speech' has not proved the panacea that was hoped. Attention is now being directed to the 'neglected situation' in the development of oral language with the focus on interaction. Cazden (1970) has considered the relevance of the topic, the task and the listener

17

to the quantity and complexity of language elicited. Although erroneous conclusions would be reached by any attempt to identify print with speech written down, it would, however, be accurate to describe print as also a form of communication and to consider the extent to which, and the ways in which, the recent studies of language have implications for the teacher of reading. As in oral language, so in reading, it seems important that the 'neglected situation' be considered and that reading be analysed as a means of communication or as a 'psycholinguistic guessing game' (Goodman 1970). Too much attention has been directed to reading readiness as requiring an analysis of skills which appear likely to have relevance in the reading situation and too little attention to the reading task itself. It is important for the beginning reading teacher to turn her attention to a 'sensitive observation of reading behaviour' (Clay 1972) and to 'a clear understanding of what the skilled reader can do and of what the beginning reader is trying to do' Smith (1971).

The teacher who approaches the early instruction in reading as the teaching of a communication skill, with silent reading as the extraction of the author's meaning, and oral reading as its communication to others, will appreciate the importance of context; she will be lead to consider the role of errors as 'miscues', some of which may indeed be indicative of progress in the development of the skill; the importance of the choice of reading material in the early stages, some materials encouraging the appropriate strategies of prediction in a language context and others to inappropriate techniques. She will be led to consider how much of the information for reading comprehension comes from the printed page and the extent to which comprehension must *precede* rather than follow the identification of individual words. In short, the teacher who considers reading as a communication skill will use a very different approach from the teacher for whom reading is decoding to spoken language.

It seems important to approach the teaching of reading from an analysis of the skills and knowledge the child has already acquired when he begins learning to read and to consider the additional knowledge and skills required for fluent reading. Such an analysis may prevent the teacher from developing an approach which might mistakenly emphasize a precision of visual scanning of words or of letters which might indeed be detrimental to the efficient development of fluent reading. Similarly an emphasis on precision in auditory discrimination may also be inappropriate. The skill crucial for reading tapped by the well-known tests of auditory discrimination may be a language processing one rather than that which the test purports to measure (Hardy 1973 and Blank 1970).

In a recent paper entitled 'Language and reading research trends' (Clark in press), I have considered some of the aspects of the language of the child, the teacher and the instructional materials which may be of importance to the teaching of reading. In the remainder of this present paper, an attempt will be made to consider the extent to which a study of children who were already fluent readers on commencing school can throw light on some of the crucial variables in the teaching situation.

In common with many other psychologists, I had made a study of the characteristics of children who had severe and prolonged difficulty in learning to read (Clark 1970). That investigation was a community-based study of 1,544 children at seven years of age. Those children who had still not achieved any independent reading skill at that age were over a period of years studied in detail. It was appreciated, however, that such a study would not make it possible to distinguish those factors which had caused the reading failure from others which were associated with it or caused by the failure. For such an analysis it was necessary to study children from the age at which they started school and attempt to identify factors which were predictive of children who were 'at risk'. Such a study has been in progress for the last three years. It was felt, however, that studies such as these, while possibly helping to determine causation *within* the school situation, would not isolate any factors which might be specific to the group-class situation within school in which most children learn to read and distinguish them from others which might be intrinsic to the reading situation. A study of young fluent readers might shed some light on the development of skilled reading in ways that might otherwise have been overlooked.

For that reason an additional study was undertaken of children who were already fluent readers on commencing school at five years of age. The study has in some ways confirmed present beliefs on the crucial variables in learning to read and has also produced general findings in line with those of Durkin (1966) and Torrey (1973). There are, however, some significant characteristics of these present children and their families which are worthy of consideration by beginning reading teachers. It is with these aspects that this paper is concerned.

Aims of the study

The aim of the study was to determine the particular *strengths and weaknesses* of children who learnt to read at an early age without the assistance of the school.

Focus only on children who learn to read within a range of methods and with the materials available in schools may lead to overemphasis on some aspects of the children's development and may lead us to regard these as intrinsically significant to learning to read. The study of children for whom learning to read was speedy, effortless and an enjoyable task achieved in an informal, unstructured setting should, it was felt, contribute to the understanding of the process of learning to read.

A study of the deficits in the homes of children who fail in reading may lead to unjustified conclusions regarding the inevitable consequences of such circumstances. The aim in studying the home background of these children was not only to ascertain the strengths, but also the weaknesses *in spite of* which they had learnt to read at an early age.

The sample

A request was sent round schools in the Glasgow area in 1969/70 asking for referral of any child who on starting school was already a fluent reader, and this was followed by further requests in 1971 and 72. The criterion for inclusion in the study was that the child on testing could read at least twenty-five words on the Schonell Graded Word Reading Test and only such children were retained for further study. That is, these children had already an independent reading skill on beginning school. It was hoped that the children would be referred as soon as possible after commencing school, but there was on occasion a time lag—particularly with the first children referred. The age range of the children on initial testing was 4 years 9 months to 6 years 4 months and contact with the children has been maintained up to the present time—the oldest are now nine years of age. Thirty-two children have been studied. Four of the girls were from a selective school which was approached directly; a school in which it is a common occurrence to have children enter school either reading fluently or beginning to read. The remaining twenty-eight children (twenty boys and eight girls) were from twenty-four different schools, and from widely different backgrounds.

It cannot be claimed that this is a total sample of such children attending schools in the Glasgow area over the period in question as no attempt was made to screen the population. Other schools may have failed to refer children who were as advanced as these children. For some of the schools who did refer children, however, these were the only such children they had experienced in a number of years. No attempt was made to establish a control group of children as was done in Durkin's study. This study has been an intensive analysis of the strengths and weaknesses of these children, of their schools and their attitudes to such children, and of their family backgrounds. In as far as the characteristics of the group in general appear to be comparable to those found by Durkin and others it seems legitimate, however, to consider that such are representative of children who read early. In addition to testing of the children on a wide range of psychological tests, the parents have been interviewed on at least two occasions—when the children started school and again recently.

The investigation

Reading
The initial testing of reading was on the Schonell Graded Word Reading Test which was later supplemented by the Neale Analysis of Reading Ability. The range of reading ages may be seen in tables 1 and 2 below. An interesting characteristic of some of the most fluent readers was the artificiality for them of an oral reading task such as the Neale, since clearly their preferred mode of reading was silently. Some of the mothers had indeed been astonished to realize that their children were reading and they had not at first appreciated how much the children had progressed.

This should not lead one to underestimate the role of an adult for each of these children in directing the child's attention to the precise cues to be extracted in order to obtain meaning from print, by reading to the child and answering questions immediately, precisely and on the level appropriate

Table 1 WPPSI Full Scale IQs and Schonell Reading Ages* of thirty-two fluent readers

SRA* in yrs.	WPPSI full-scale IQs						
	90+	100+	110+	120+	130+	140+	Totals
11+				1	2		3
10+		1	2	2	3	1	9
9+			5	1			6
8+	1	2	3	1	3	1	11
7+		1		1	1		3
Totals	1	4	10	6	9	2	32

Table 2 Neale Reading Ages (Accuracy) and Daniels Spelling Ages* of thirty-two fluent readers

DSA* in yrs.	Neale Reading Ages in years					
	7+	8+	9+	10+	11+	Totals
12+				1		1
11+					1	1
10+						—
9+			5	1	1	7
8+		1	5	3		9
7+	1	3	5	1		10
6+	1	1	1			3
5+		1				1
Totals	2	6	16	6	2	32

to that particular child's needs at the moment.

Although a love of books was evident in many of the homes, not all had an extensive collection of either children's or of adult's books. Few of the children had learnt to read from a reading scheme though where there was an older brother or sister the books thus made available were often utilized. For some, the initial focus had been television advertisements, often reinforced on visits to the supermarket, cars and garage signs. In other words print in the environment was sensitively observed in whatever manner it appeared. The initial motivation appeared often to have come from the child but the continuing stimulation, encouragement and reinforcement was clearly present from at least one adult in the house. For many of the girls the acquisition of reading skill provided a possibility for rereading stories which had previously been read to them, or further books by the same author, and certainly books in which a concerned parent might well have encouraged an interest. A different pattern was apparent in the development of reading skills in many of the boys. The boys were much less interested in fiction initially and more interested in extending their knowledge in areas, say science for example, which would have been regarded as beyond the capacity of children of their age. Encyclopedias, dictionaries and other reference books held a fascination for many of these boys as did nature programmes, quiz programmes and any types of word puzzle games on television. It is difficult to generalize about many characteristics of these children since they showed such a range of skills, interests and even personality and home background. This striking difference in the preferred reading materials of the boys and girls was still apparent recently when their present interest in reading and related skills was explored. One nine year old boy, interested in chess, has also become interested in Latin because he wished to translate Latin quotations in Jennings books he was reading and he is now working with the assistance and encouragement of his headmaster. Another boy aged only seven is interested in chess and taught himself the moves and chess notation using his reading skill to advance this interest—his father who learnt chess to try and play with him admits to being the less successful. The parents of this same boy in order to allay his fear of thunder, obtained a book on storms which they were intending to read to him. He had himself found and read the book, and, developed an interest in studying this further, books being a natural source of this further knowledge. Many more examples could be quoted of interests in other children in the sample supported and further stimulated by the parents. The local library had become a valuable source of reading material for most of these children but where the child's interests were too advanced or their families were unable to give guidance as well as support, the situation could be rather frustrating. In many libraries, and indeed in some schools, age was a barrier which prevented access either to the fiction or reference books they wished to read. In few libraries was there any member of staff who had helped to develop the talents of these children. Many of these parents were members of the local library and could both help and guide the children and if necessary borrow books to suit the child's taste but in some instances it was sad to see the potential not being developed because a family did not know how to obtain further guidance for their child. It is easy to dismiss these children and say that many of them were gifted—some certainly were as measured by an intelligence test. Already, however, intelligence tests are being questioned as measures of innate ability and the extent to which they are a combination of innate potential and environment enrichment must be considered. Indeed, the Stanford Binet Intelligence Test is being used in some preschool intervention studies not only as a base line, but also as a measure of the effectiveness of the programme. It is important therefore, not to dismiss the language development or the development of the reading skill and interest of these children as either the result of specific skills or innate potential but to question which characteristics of their environment had assisted this precocious development.

Spelling

All of the children on initial testing could already spell some words on the Daniels Spelling Test. For most, not only reading, but also writing had early been of interest. Many children have blackboards and chalks but for these children such materials were of particular interest. Significant features in their spelling were first that their errors were an interesting approximation to English and second that the children were frequently aware of the words they could not spell.

The following are examples of these children's misspellings on the Daniels Test:

any	anee, eny, eni, ani, enye, eanyi.
fight	fite, fitgh, fiet, fihgt, figth.
answer	anser, ansir, ansur, ansr, awnser, anwser, answr.
beautiful	butfle, buateatfoal, butifu, buetfell, bewtifull.

Here, as in reading, it seems important that the teacher observe the errors and the extent to which they indicate a progressive development of miscues towards an implicit awareness of English spelling patterns. The beginning of such awareness was apparent even in the children in this group who were as yet able to spell only a few words. In short, an awareness of the characteristics of the written English language was developing in these children, though many of them would have been quite unable to verbalize the distinctions which were implicit in their behaviour. In determining a young child's grasp of the characteristics of print, it seems important not to assume a lack of appreciation where the child is unable to verbalize the meaning of a letter, a word, a sound; such a child may still be able to appreciate the crucial features of the language.

On the negative side one aspect which was noted in some of these children was the poor motor coordination with which they produced their 'good' spelling. It is important to bear in mind the fact that within such a group there will be a range of levels of motor coordination and that because a child can read and even spell fluently (coupled in some cases with high intelligence) this does not mean that if he tries he can write or play games on a commensurate level. Indeed one parent recently remarked that the teacher was amused that a child who could read on that level was still having difficulties in tying his shoe laces at the age of seven.

Arithmetic

This was tested only within the context of a subtest in the Wechsler Primary and Preschool Intelligence Scale (WPPSI). On that test, however, most of the children made scores which were well above average. The verbal context in which the questions are posed should be considered, however, since this may be one explanation for their high scores. Several of the children were, however, fascinated by numbers and very gifted in their ability to deal with large numbers. The skills displayed by these children highlighted the importance of not assuming that all children who get sums wrong need easier sums! Several of these children with a gift for numerical computation were indeed bored with arithmetic in school and were therefore not appearing at the top of the class nor getting all their sums correct—a characteristic which was also shown by some in reading. One child who, at the age of six could add large numbers in his head, which adults had to write down to check, could not follow the written form of simple addition with carrying; while another child who could at home, without instruction, do his older sister's sums was in trouble for taking the wrong sum cards at school (harder ones). Another child aged six showed his grasp of numbers by drawing and describing a scale for weighing elephants whose indicator ran from 25 stone to 43 stone with a pointer at 26 st. 2 lbs. as the weight of that particular elephant.

In short, even when first seen, the attainments of few of these children were specific to the reading situation. All children were interviewed on several occasions and, particularly on their initial visit, it was clear how ready and eager they were to learn from a new experience. A number of the children, though not all, were of high intelligence but there were certain types of language tasks on which they made high scores. One feature which has been characteristic of the parents' attitudes on the occasions they have been interviewed, both when the child started school and recently, has been a positive, accepting, appreciative attitude to the school. They have all shown an awareness of the fact that their child was only one in a large class and that the school 'knows best'. Even where they have made comments about aspects of their child's attainment which could perhaps have been more fully catered for, this has never been in negative terms. The attitude of the parents to their children's attainment on starting school was, however, frequently one of self-conscious embarrassment. Few had mentioned to the school their child's level on starting school, most had been worried rather than pleased at their child's early interest in print. Several commented that they knew that this would confuse the child on reaching school and make it more difficult for the teacher. One parent of a very bright child observed that at first she tried to stop her daughter until she finally realized that this was not possible, and felt consoled that the child had started so early that she would be beyond the dangerous stage before starting school. Another parent when assuring me she had not been the initiator, pointed out that as she knew her child was going to an ita school, she realized that this might cause problems. Still another parent told me how her neighbour had commented on her child's attainment and, to her intense embarrassment, had insisted that she must be sitting over the child, forcing her and that she should let her play! This impression of guilt and embarrassment on the part of the parents at their children's impressive attainments on commencing school is similar to the impression gained by Durkin during her parental interviews. This should make one consider what we desire in the child commencing school—ready but not too ready; fluent but not too fluent; knowledgeable but not too knowledgeable.

The range of attainments shown by these children on starting school together with their motivation, powers of concentration and attention to detail, should make one consider further the characteristics of the children themselves and also the features in the home environment which were significant in their development. In few instances was there another child in these families who was also reading fluently on starting school. While the child under study may have had specific skills which led to the early precocious development of fluent readings, the language awareness and positive stimulating environment was a family characteristic and was not specific to that particular child. The parental interviews revealed the extent to which at least one, and often both parents regarded their role in their children's development as an interesting and rewarding experience. They showed an awareness of their children's strengths, weaknesses and individual differences which they were able to verbalize often in graphic terms. Not all the parents had experienced higher education and indeed a number had left school at the earliest age possible. Most of these had, however, a desire that their family should have, and benefit from, the experiences they had rejected or missed. Most of the parents interviewed while playing down their own part in stimulating their children's interests showed that they regarded themselves as crucially involved in their children's development. The children in these families were, it was felt, entering school interested, alert, motivated and 'ready' in many ways which would lead them to ask the appropriate questions, make the appropriate responses and develop quickly an appreciation of the essential characteristics of print.

It is important to consider the extent to which it is possible to provide in school the necessary language interaction for children less fortunate in their home circumstances. Otherwise the child deprived of the essential characteristics of language prior to and parallel to his school experiences might indeed suffer both a deprived language environment at home and a deprived language environment at school. The animated, colourful language of these parents, their absorption in their families and their positive attitude to education whatever their own educational background were at least as striking as any interest in books. For these children books were part of a language experience, an extension of it rather than an escape from other experiences. It might be salutary to consider the extent to which a background such as was to be found in the homes of these children is a crucial but overlooked factor in the apparent successes of the early instruction in reading of many other children. This one would suspect was true for example of the other children in these families.

The effects of home background on motivation and receptivity to the instruction provided by the school are frequently mentioned. It may be that deficiencies in language teaching in the schools are less apparent where the parents are providing a richness and variety of language stimulation and interaction which may be an essential component in the successful teaching of reading. The detailed findings of the present study of fluent readers will be reported elsewhere. What seemed crucial in this present paper was to highlight the extent to which they reinforce the need to look upon the development of reading as a 'patterning of complex behaviour' within a language context.

References

BLANK, M. (1970) 'Some philosophical influences underlying preschool intervention for disadvantaged children' in F. Williams (Ed) *Language and Poverty* Chicago: Markham

CAZDEN, C. B. (1970) 'The neglected situation in child language research and education' in F. Williams (Ed) *Language and Poverty* Chicago: Markham

CLARK, M. M. (1970) *Reading Difficulties in Schools* Harmondworth: Penguin

CLARK, M. M. (in press) 'Language and reading research trends' in A. Davies (Ed) *The Problems of Language and Learning* London: Heinemann

CLAY, M. M. (1972) *Reading: The Patterning of Complex Behaviour* London: Heinemann

DURKIN, D. (1966) *Children who Read Early* Columbia, New York: Teachers' College Press

HARDY, M. I. (1973) 'The development of beginning reading skills: recent findings' in M. M. Clark and A. Milne (Eds) *Reading and Related Skills* London: Ward Lock Educational

SMITH, F. (1971) *Understanding Reading* New York: Holt, Rinehart and Winston

TORREY, J. W. (1973) 'Learning to read without a teacher: a case study' in F. Smith (Ed) *Psycholinguistics and Reading* New York: Holt, Rinehart and Winston

3 The child's concepts of language

John Downing

Thought and language

Perhaps Piaget's greatest contribution to practical improvements in education has been his persistent demonstration of the need to be suspicious of all adult 'commonsense' assumptions about children's behaviour. For example, Piaget's (1959) studies of the language and thought of children have taught us to be cautious in drawing conclusions about what a child knows or understands from observations of his actions or speech. For instance, the child may be able to say 'three sevens are twenty-one' without having any of the relevant number concepts. Thus, what the child *says* about numbers may tell us nothing about his mathematical *knowledge*. Or the child may be able to use his speech apparatus to produce sounds like 'cat', 'cot', and 'cut' without any awareness or understanding that he is manipulating the vowel sound only. Thus what the child *does* in activating his vocal apparatus tells us nothing about his linguistic *knowledge*. In summary we must not assume that the child has the corresponding concept just because he can say the word for it or perform some action which appears to reflect its use.

In learning the skills of reading and writing it seems most probable that the child has to become aware of certain aspects of spoken language which he has not previously perceived. For example, in order to write *fish and chips* or *bread and jam* correctly he needs to understand the concept of word. Previously he heard and said 'fishnchips' and 'breadnjam'. Similarly (though much more difficult), although the child is quite capable of saying and hearing 'jam' and can easily tell it apart from 'ham', to spell them phonically he must understand first the concept of phoneme (minimum sound unit) and second the way in which phonemes follow one another in a special order in time. Then he can write *j*, followed by *a*, and then *m*. This becomes even more important in his free writing when he wants to write more difficult words or new words such as 'yam'.

It is concepts like these—word and phoneme—which seem to be essential to the child's thinking about the tasks of learning *how to* read and *how to* write. In psychology we use the technical term 'cognition' to describe this category of mental behaviour which in everyday speech is called 'knowing' and 'understanding'. Thus 'cognitive learning' means the act of getting to know or understand something. In teaching children to read and write we are trying to develop their cognitive clarity about these skills. We want them to know and understand how to read and how to write and all the many other 'how tos' which they will meet on their way to developing the whole complex skill.

Early linguistic concepts

What has been said in the previous section is not only theory. A fair amount of evidence has accumulated to show that the very nub of the problem of learning to read lies in this development of cognitive clarity.

The earliest research clues to this finding were found in the studies of M. D. Vernon (1957) in England and Vygotsky (1962, but written in Russian much earlier) in the USSR.

Vernon made a comprehensive international review of the research on causes of reading disability. She concluded from her extensive survey and intensive psychological analysis of all the data, 'Thus the fundamental and basic characteristic of reading disability appears to be cognitive confusion.' She explains this cognitive aspect as follows. The child who has failed in reading is 'hopelessly uncertain and confused as to why certain successions of printed letters should correspond to certain phonetic sounds in words.' Vernon emphasized that the reading disabled child 'does not seem to understand why' written language is what it is.

Vygotsky's contribution is more specific. His research on literacy acquisition in Russian children led him to just two conclusions. First, 'it is the abstract quality of written language that is the main stumbling block', and, second, the child 'has little motivation to learn writing when we begin to teach it. He feels no need for it and has only a vague idea of its usefulness.' This second point of Vygotsky's specifies one of the chief concepts which is absolutely essential if the child is to become a reader or a writer, that is, the concept of the function of written language—*why* people read and *why* people write.

The real breakthrough in this research came quite recently when Jessie Reid (1966) published her classic article 'Learning to think about reading'. In Piaget-type interviews with five year old beginners in a Scottish primary school, Reid explored what children think language and reading are. She found that such young children have quite different concepts to the ones adults tend to take for granted. She confirmed Vygotsky's conclusion that the beginner does not possess the fundamental concept of the functions of reading and writing. Reid reported that to these Scottish children, reading 'is a mysterious activity, to which they come with only the vaguest of expectancies'. Reid added to our knowledge of this problem in her finding that her subjects 'had very little precise notion of what the activity consisted in'.

The present author (Downing, 1970) replicated Reid's study. Similar interviews were conducted, but this time with English children from a primary school near London. The children, of course, expressed themselves in different individual ways but the conclusions confirmed Reid's earlier findings. These conclusions were further strengthened by the fact that the studies in England did not rely on what children *said* about language and reading. A series of games and experiments were devised in which the children could demonstrate their knowledge and understanding of the concepts which are basic tools for thinking about why people read and how they do it. It made some difference but not much. The results left no room for doubt. *The normal state of the young child taking his first steps in learning to read is one of cognitive confusion about these basic concepts of language.*

The English five year olds were followed through their first year in the infant department and it was possible to study their cognitive development. It became clear that their progress in learning to read depended on *their growth in cognitive clarity* (Downing 1972). The more they understood why and how people read and write the better was their progress in learning these skills. With their growth in understanding came clearer concepts of such linguistic categories as word and phoneme. Their knowledge of the labels for these categories lagged behind their understanding. They knew what a phoneme was before they could describe it or label it—which is exactly what we should expect from more general psychological research on child thought and language. As Piaget (1959) has said, 'Verbal forms evolve more slowly than actual understanding.'

In the last few years psychologists in several countries have become interested in children's concepts of language, with the result that we now have rather strong evidence for the importance of cognitive clarity in learning to read. Meltzer and Herse (1969) in the United States used a number of methods to test American school beginners' concept of the written word. For example, they gave each child a sentence printed on a card and a pair of scissors with the spoken request 'please cut me off a word'. Sometimes a child did cut off a word, but it was just as likely that the child's 'word' would be half a word or more than a word. Kingston, Weaver, and Figa (1972) conducted a series of experiments designed to investigate American children's conceptions of both spoken word and written word. They concluded, 'These five experiments demonstrate quite conclusively that first grade children lack precise concepts concerning the nature of "a word".' In Canada, Downing and Oliver (in press) improved the technique for testing a child's concept of spoken word to make sure that the young beginner understood the instruction of the tester better. But the result was the same, thus confirming that Canadian children begin in the same normal state of cognitive confusion in this respect as do Scottish, English and American beginners. Another study in Canada has related this investigation of children's linguistic concepts to the teacher's practical concern for reading readiness. Evanechko, Ollila, Downing and Braum (1973) constructed a new reading readiness battery which includes a paper and pencil test of several concepts of written language. Results of the tests indicate that the child's development of these concepts is an important factor in reading readiness.

Two other research studies have related children's concepts of language to growth. Lansdown and Davis (1972) used Reid's (1966) original interview method and Downing's (1970) first experimental testing technique to compare twenty-four normal children with thirty ESN pupils. Lansdown and Davis found that 'the trends shown before were repeated' with the normal children, but that 'consistent patterns of cognitive clarity' did not show 'until the age of nine or so' in the ESN pupils. Hazel Francis (1973) conducted a series of tests of the language concepts, vocabulary, and reading achievement of fifty boys and girls in a Leeds primary school. She found that her highest correlation (.41) was between reading and technical vocabulary about language. When she statistically controlled general vocabulary skill the correlation was still considerable (.34), 'indicating that factors independent of a general ability to deal with abstract concepts were involved in learning technical vocabulary, and that these were closely related to the reading process'. This seems to suggest that there are *specific* concepts of language which are important in learning how to read. Some of these specific concepts are known from the research reviewed above e.g. *word, phoneme, sentence, reading, writing, letter* and so on. Others may be guessed at, now that research has put us on the track of the importance of learning concepts of language in developing the skills of reading and writing.

Practical implications
If these specific linguistic concepts are so important in learning to read, teachers will want to find ways of helping children to develop a clear understanding of them. But the teaching of concepts is full of pitfalls. The most common and dangerous trap is the temptation to tell. We should remember the examples given earlier in this paper. If the child has learned to recite 'three sevens are twenty-one' there is no guarantee that he understands what he is saying or knows the corresponding number concepts. In fact, telling may be worse than useless because, when the child learns to recite words he does not understand, he learns something in addition which works against our purpose. He may learn to believe, 'I don't understand these things. I'm no good at it.' Thus a barrier to understanding can be created by teachers who try to save time by telling.

The key to effective concept learning is the provision of experiences which first, stir the child's curiosity, and second provide sufficient reliable information for discovery of the concept. The child's curiosity will be stirred if the language activities provided are relevant to his needs and interests. The sufficiency and reliability of the information contained in those activities depend on the teacher's planning and resources.

The most important thing of all is for the teacher herself to be clear about the linguistic concepts involved in learning to read. Unfortunately, the training of teachers has been so woefully inadequate in this respect that there is a real danger that many teachers have not thought out what linguistic concepts children need to learn in developing the skills of reading and writing. Probably, at the present time many children are learning these concepts like nonswimmers thrown in at the deep end of a swimming pool.

This is indicated by several comments included in Hazel Francis's (1973) article. She noted that, when children talked to her about language, 'The outstanding feature was the almost universal reference to spelling, reading and writing. Almost no replies indicated an awareness of the use of words or sentences in the spoken language.' Therefore, Francis concluded that the children 'derived the concepts *word* and *sentence* from their mastery of reading and writing. . . .' Francis also states that the 'children developed an analytical approach to spoken language while they were engaged in learning to read'. But the crux of the problem is indicated by Francis's perception of the child's floundering in the deep end of the reading swimming pool:

> It was as though the children had never thought to analyse speech, but in learning to read had been forced to recognize units and subdivisions. The use of words like *letter, word* and *sentence* in teaching was not so much a direct aid to instruction but a challenge to find their meaning.

That is the way it is. And who knows how many children fail in reading because of the deep end immersion in a sea of undefined linguistic concepts.

Some new ways
Between 1969 and 1972 a team of specialists from fourteen countries worked together to study the universal characteristics of learning to read and write in varying cultures and differing languages. The results were published recently in a book *Comparative Reading* (Downing 1973). One of the outstanding contributions to this cooperative study came from the USSR. Elkonin's report on that country describes in detail a method used with Russian children to help them to become aware of the concept of phoneme in spoken language and to understand how a word consists of a group of phonemes arranged in a special order in time.

Elkonin (1973) recognizes the adult's failure to appreciate the child's difficulties in understanding these apparently simple concepts:

> The arrangement of a succession of sounds in a word, as well as the discrimination of a single sound in a word, seems an extraordinarily simple act for a normal literate adult. This illusion arises from the fact that, at this higher level of development, the operation occurs by then as abbreviated, generalized, perfected, and automatic mental behaviour, which requires no effort and causes no problems. But the truth is that this is only the final form of the process of the sound analysis of a word.

Elkonin goes on to describe 'a method for materializing the sound structure of words' which bears some resemblance to the kind of activities which English primary schools have developed to provide concrete experiences of exemplars of mathematical and scientific concepts in recent years. Space does not permit a description here of these Russian methods for developing children's concepts of language. Elkonin's report provides full detail of the teaching techniques, the apparatus, and the research evidence in support of the method.

Recently, Elkonin's method was adapted for the English language and tested in an experiment with Canadian children. The results are encouraging. Ollila, Johnson, and Downing (in press) found that Elkonin's method not only improved five year olds' concepts of the phoneme, but it also created superior reading readiness in comparison with children taught by two other well-known American reading readiness schemes.

However, the method itself may not be Elkonin's chief contribution. The great potential in his work is its clear demonstration of what it is the child needs to know and understand about these particular linguistic concepts. Teachers who study or try Elkonin's method are likely to become better teachers of reading because of their clearer understanding of the problems which the child must solve in developing these basic conceptual tools of the tasks of learning how to read and write.

References

DOWNING, J. (1970) Children's concepts of language in learning to read *Educational Research* 12, 106-112

DOWNING, J. (1972) Children's developing concepts of spoken and written language *Journal of Reading Behavior* 4, 1-19

DOWNING, J. (1973) *Comparative Reading* London: Collier-Macmillan

DOWNING, J. and OLIVER, P. (in press) The child's conception of a word *Reading Research Quarterly*

ELKONIN, D. B. (1973) 'USSR' in J. Downing *Comparative Reading* London: Collier-Macmillan

EVANECHKO, P., OLLILA, L., DOWNING, J. and BRAUN, C. (1973) An investigation of the reading readiness domain *Research in the Teaching of English* 7, 61-78

FRANCIS, H. (1973) Children's experience of reading and notions of units in language *British Journal of Educational Psychology* 43, 17-23

KINGSTON, A. J., WEAVER, W. W. and FIGA, L. E. (1972) 'Experiments in children's perceptions of words and word boundaries' in F. P. Greene (Ed) *Investigations Relating to Mature Reading* Milwaukee, Wisc.: National Reading Conference Incorporated

LANSDOWN, R. and DAVIS, V. (1972) The language of reading and the ESN child *Reading* 6, 21-24

MELTZER, N. S. and HERSE, R. (1969) The boundaries of written words as seen by first graders *Journal of Reading Behavior* 1, 3-14

OLLILA, L., JOHNSON, T. and DOWNING, J. (in press) The effects of Russian methods of auditory discrimination on English speaking children in Canada *Journal of Educational Research*

PIAGET, J. (1959) *The Language and Thought of the Child* (3rd revised edition) London: Routledge and Kegan Paul

REID, J. F. (1966) Learning to think about reading *Educational Research* 9, 56-62

VERNON, M. D. (1957) *Backwardness in Reading* London: Cambridge University Press

VYGOTSKY, L. S. (1962) *Thought and Language* Cambridge, Mass.: M.I.T. Press

B

4 Games for reading readiness

Elizabeth Hunter

The topic of reading readiness provides a wide area of interest and controversy for all those who are concerned with the education of young children, and requires no discussion here. In using the word 'games' in this context, my intention is to differentiate between free play, which is entirely pupil-initiated, and activities which are considerably more teacher-initiated but equally enjoyable for the child.

The British infant school has achieved an international reputation for the success of its child-centred methods, and for the emphasis given to the fostering of creativity in our young pupils. The provision of play materials like sand, water, clay, paints etc is generally excellent, and few, if any, educationists underrate the value of learning through free play. In the USA during the 1940s and 50s some debate surrounded the practice of 'free' classroom methods. There was criticism on the grounds that many pupils were making inadequate progress, especially in reading. Some critics attributed this to misinterpretation of the educational philosophy of John Dewey, and Dewey himself had attempted to clarify his position in his last book, published in 1938:

> Some teachers seem to be afraid even to make suggestions to the members of a group as to what they should do. I have heard of cases in which the children are surrounded with objects and materials, and then left entirely to themselves, the teacher being loath to suggest even what might be done with the materials lest freedom be impinged upon.

Certainly Dewey was discussing slightly older children in the context of skill learning rather than personality growth, but I should like to suggest that a very small measure of this criticism may be relevant to our infant education. Of more general relevance is Dewey's lifelong belief in the dangers of treating alternative policies as if they were irretrievably dichotomous. Teaching methods need not be *either* pupil-centred *or* teacher-centred; classrooms need not be *either* formal *or* free. It is more meaningful to envisage a continuum between two extremes, and to consider the use of a variety of approaches which may relate to different points along the continuum. The achievement of dissimilar educational objectives requires the use of differing strategies and materials, and while the concept of freedom is essential in the context of freedom for personality growth, it is less acceptable in the sense of providing freedom from the necessity of learning basic skills. A great deal has been written about what constitutes basic skills and which of these, if any, may appropriately begin in the infant school. My premise is the general recognition of the crucial importance of language skills to any definition of reading readiness, and in this area, Bruner's (1960) hypothesis that 'the foundations of any subject may be taught to anybody at any age in some form' can be enlisted to support my view that most of the games which will be discussed can be adapted for use with nursery school pupils.

In her paper entitled 'Talking, thinking and learning', Jessie Reid is concerned with the development of the kind of language which is a 'logical tool', essential for communicating thought, classifying, conveying precise information and describing processes. She suggests that (Reid 1967):

> This development can take place only in a teaching and learning situation where talk is the order of the day—not just idle chatter, and not conventional questioning by the teacher and answering by the class, but something much more like real 'dialogue', entered into by both sides on an equal footing.

In practical terms this would demand from the teacher an understanding of the aims and objectives of a language extension programme, knowledge of the techniques required to encourage children to listen, question and discuss, and—above all—a great deal of time. Providing language activities to meet the individual needs of thirty small pupils is a daunting task, and consequently the use of language games which facilitate less closely supervised learning are extremely helpful, if not essential. It is not suggested that language games should replace free play activities. Each child requires his own professionally balanced diet, and games involving language usage are at least as important as any others, and for a majority of our inner-city and immigrant children it can be argued that they are significantly more important.

In Britain during the last few years, heads of schools and teachers have involved themselves in creating, designing, preparing and testing language games for young children. Meeting in teachers centres, this blending of expertise, enthusiasm and cooperative effort has generated sources of materials on which games can be based, and from which others can be adapted. Adaptation is generally found to be important, because the most valuable games must meet the needs of the individual teacher in catering for her particular pupils.

Since 1970 the Primary Extension Programme of the Council for Educational Technology has been sponsoring experimentation with language games which can be used by children from the age of three. With the cooperation of local education authorities, this has entailed special in-service training courses for 10 per cent of the early childhood educators in twelve districts of urban and rural deprivation throughout the United Kingdom. Teachers' 'workshop' sessions have resulted in the production of a variety of materials which demand the minimum of supervision, thus enabling pupils to have much more language experience in terms of time allocation, encouraging them to take some responsibility for their own learning, and freeing the teacher to distribute her attention among groups and individuals. Games recorded on cassettes include *Listening for Pleasure* stories incorporating music and rhymes, and 'instruction stories', during which pupils are invited to arrange cut-outs on a flannelgraph or teaslegraph board. To exploit local interests, the *Down your Way* series illustrates the results achieved by a group of infants in a Glasgow Gorbals school, who were allowed to use a simple Instamatic camera during a supervised walk in the immediate neighbourhood. Discussion of the enlarged photographs stimulated talk among the children, which was recorded as a guide for vocabulary games. The photographs also became the basis for a language-experience approach to beginning reading.

Most of the PEP games are described as useful 'starters' which the teacher can readily adapt, and all the materials are intended to be incorporated into the individual teacher's overall scheme.

The Inner London Education Authority's Centre for Urban Educational Studies (CUES) is also exploring games which facilitate autonomous group study for very young pupils. The Centre's Language Division is directed by Jim Wright, whose 'workshop' seminars with heads of schools and teachers have resulted in the production of a series of games called 'Listen, Discuss and Do'. A set of graded scripts is available for recording onto audio tapes or cassettes. Personal recording gives the teacher freedom to make decisions about whether to record her own voice or to record a variety of voices. It also solves the problem relating to prerecorded material and regional dialects. The games are played in groups of three or four. Each player has a work book, which is an integral part of the game, and one child is appointed as controller of the machine's 'playback' button. The recording poses a series of puzzles or tasks which involve the group in discussion and decision-making, and the controller is asked to 'switch off' while each section of the game is completed. Small groups of nursery and infant pupils can become happily and usefully absorbed in these activities for up to fifteen minutes in the initial stages, and for longer periods as the programmed games develop systematically over a period of time.

Talk Reform by Denis and Georgina Gahagan (1971) is an account of their London East End research project in the field of early language development. The games used for their experimentation are described in chapter four of the book, and were devised to give infants training and practice in listening, discussing, and communicating with confidence, fluency and accuracy. The children play in pairs or in small groups, and many of these games require continuous teacher involvement. In the original project the Gahagans asked for twenty minutes of daily participation in the games, and even this small allocation of time proved beneficial.

A source of valuable material for group study or individual pupil study is to be found in the BBC Schools Broadcasting Radio series entitled

Listening and Reading. Stages 1 and 2 are suitable for prereading and early reading levels, each stage comprising ten stories of ten minutes duration. These are intended to be recorded during transmission. Books containing the printed versions of the stories and used in conjunction with the tapes or cassettes, are well produced and surprisingly inexpensive. No illustrations are used with the stories, which are selected and adapted by Philippa Pearce, and cater for a wide variety of tastes.

> *Listening and Reading* is an attempt to supply material that the children will want to read; material of such power and vigour that the message will carry the medium into their minds. The real message will be that these ciphers on paper are the key to entertainment and learning.

In 1971-72, the CET Primary Extension Programme carried out empirical research into the effects of using *Listening and Reading*. Three schools in areas of urban deprivation were involved, and reception class infants were permitted to listen to their favourite stories whenever opportunities arose (there were three cassette playback machines in each classroom). It was found that they listened to a story ten times on average. During the first term, teachers noted that many children were using vocabulary derived from the stories. In the second term more pupils began to read than in previous years, and during the third term language from the stories was noticeably incorporated into the children's own creative writing.

My own current empirical research in the field of reading readiness has enabled me to work with gifted and enthusiastic teachers in testing, adapting, grading, observing and recording the effects of most of the games which have been described in this paper. The work is rewarding and exciting, and it is my belief that the systematic use of games for reading readiness may have important implications for the curricula of nursery and infant schools. As Smith, Goodman and Meredith (1970) claim in *Language and Thinking in the Elementary School,* 'Teaching and learning are mainly language games in which the stakes are high—a true education.'

NB   When this paper was presented at the Conference it was illustrated by audio tapes, slides and video tapes.

References
BRUNER, J. S. (1960) *The Process of Education* New York: Vintage Books
DEWEY, J. (1938) *Experience and Education* New York: Macmillan
GAHAGAN, D. M. and GAHAGAN, G. A. (1971) *Talk Reform* London: University of London Press
REID, J. F. (1967) Talking, thinking and learning *Reading* 1, 1, 5-9
SMITH, E. B., GOODMAN, H. and MEREDITH, (1970) *Language and Thinking in the Elementary Schools* New York: Holt, Rinehart and Winston

Sources

BBC Schools Broadcasting Council The Langham, Portland Place, London
W1A 1AA

Centre for Urban Educational Studies Language Division, 34 Aberdeen
Park, London N5

5 Building a sound foundation for literacy

Joyce M. Morris

Introduction

Teachers have many responsibilities, but none is greater than making sure that children build a sound foundation for literacy during their early schooling. For, as research has shown (Morris 1966), pupils who fail to do this rarely succeed in subsequent school life or, indeed, in securing satisfactory employment on leaving school.

Some might argue that the poor prognosis for late starters can be attributed largely to our traditionally literate society which engenders inferiority feelings in young children who do not live up to expectations. Others might argue that late starters do not usually make up for lost ground because, hitherto, junior and secondary teachers have not been adequately trained to deal with their special problems.

There is more than a grain of truth in both these arguments. Nevertheless, even if the community's sights were lowered and, rightly, all teachers were equipped to develop language skills, the truth would still remain that the golden years for linguistic development are those before nine. Hence, parents and teachers of preschool and first-school children should be encouraged to utilize fully the young child's sensitive period for language learning.

Happily, encouragement for parents has been more forthcoming in recent years. The mass media have publicised the marked difference that an encouraging home background can make to a pupil's scholastic progress. And parents have been informed about ways of developing children's oracy and interest in the written word as a prelude to literacy. By the same token, unhappily, some parents have been made to feel inadequate, and a great deal still needs to be done in this area of parent education.

Parents can and do make a significant contribution. But it is teachers who are ultimately accountable for building a sound foundation for literacy. Not so long ago, this virtually meant infant teachers only. Whereas now, with the advent of first schools and the proposed extension of nursery provision, it will soon encompass teachers of children aged four to nine.

On the whole, the mass media have not treated teachers of this age group as sympathetically as they have treated parents. As I pointed out last year (Morris 1973), they have not been accorded their rightful status largely through ignorance of the explicit knowledge and expertise required to be a successful teacher of initial literacy. Paradoxically, they have been blamed for our literacy problems and, what is more, by people demonstrating scanty knowledge of their working conditions. They have also been alternatively exhorted by nonspecialists to change methods, materials or media, and to put their faith in good teacher-pupil relationships in a rich classroom environment. Furthermore, they have been urged to try an integrated day, team teaching, open-plan situations and so on. No wonder that they flock to language and literacy courses for reliable information to sort out what is likely to work best for them and their pupils! No wonder that advisory services for teachers continue to grow apace!

If all teachers had a preservice course such as I outlined at the last conference (Morris 1973), they would be more confident and better able to combat the forces of Ignorance, Confusion and Fear which I discussed the previous year (Morris 1972). Unfortunately, this is far from the case. Moreover, in my view, the situation is likely to get worse when future teacher-training courses are designed according to the pattern laid down in the recent Government White Paper *Education: A Framework for Expansion.*

In the circumstances, it might be helpful to discuss what is essentially involved in building a sound foundation for literacy, thereby highlighting the role of teachers and the support they need besides that of parents. So let us start in logical fashion with preschool considerations, paying special attention to problems and controversial issues.

Preschool oracy
Normal, hearing children born to English-speaking parents learn to understand and speak their mother tongue before the age of five. But they do not all learn the same kind of English. They learn a *dialect,* that is, a form of the language in terms of phonology, lexis and grammar peculiar to the region, social class or (in the case of West Indians) the ethnic group in which they are brought up. They also develop their own *idiolect* or idiosyncratic habits of speech such as favourite expressions.

Problems
Thus, although it is important to foster the growth of preschool oracy as a basis for literacy, it is equally important to recognize problems arising from speech differences when children are introduced to the written language. For example, some dialects make it easier and others harder to read and spell certain words. Scottish children generally pronounce vowel differences in words like 'fern', 'fir', 'worm' and 'fur'. Whereas Cockneys make no distinction and, moreover, pronounce words like 'think' as though they began with /f/. At the grammatical level, West Indian children experience a wide mismatch because of nonstandard grammatical features in their speech such as subject-verb disagreement, verbs lacking time reference, regular noun plurals not indicated by the 's' addition, no gender for the third person and so on.

There are also differences between the language of working-class and middle-class children, though these have not yet been fully documented. Moreover, the well-known theories of Bernstein have been criticised by such authorities as Coulthard (1969) and, more recently, by Rosen (1972). Finally, in our multiracial society, there are the special problems of children for whom English is a second language.

Controversial issues

Linguistic differences
The educational implications of these and other linguistic differences continue to be the subject of debate. Leaving aside the question of non-English-speaking immigrants, expert opinion seems to be divided about dialects. Some say that, because a child's speech is a very personal matter, one should not attempt to alter it to conform to standard English. Others advocate helping children to realize that, particularly in this television age, everybody should be able to understand other dialects and, preferably, to use the form of English acceptable to the international community of educated users.

With regard to class differences in language usage, style and content, authorities generally agree that lower working-class children should be helped to acquire the appropriate language base for their essential literacy even though some alienation from their backgrounds might ensue. However, they are divided as to how this should be achieved. There is resistance to structured approaches like those of Deutsch (1963), Bereiter and Engelmann (1966) and the Peabody Language Development Kits (Dunn and Smith 1967). Yet, as indicated by recent research (Thomas 1973), traditional nursery methods of child-initiated activity may not necessarily promote language development.

Aims of nursery education
Not only the methods but the aims of nursery education need reexamination. The Schools Council report (Taylor *et al* 1972) on what a national sample of nursery teachers judge these aims to be suggests that language development is not given the priority it deserves. Besides not being mentioned as a requisite of preservice training, it ranks equal fifth with physical development out of twelve objectives listed, and with a frequency of only 6.5 per cent. Therefore, unless these views can be changed, the proposed extension of nursery education is unlikely to do what it could to equip underprivileged children with adequate spoken language for a successful introduction to literacy.

According to the same report, only 4.4 per cent of the teachers' statements indicate that a valid aim of nursery schooling is to lay foundations for a child's future education. Here, prereading activities and simple word recognition each got a single mention. So, at present, the role of nursery teachers is not generally considered by them to include introducing children to reading and writing.

Initial literacy
It will be some time before there is universal nursery education, and even

then its aims may not have been oriented in favour of an emphasis on linguistic and cognitive growth. Accordingly, initial literacy will continue to be the main responsibility of first school teachers and those who decide their working conditions.

Problems
At present, the working conditions of far too many teachers are unsatisfactory. Space will allow brief discussion of only three before proceeding to other problems.

Size of classes
First, in classes of thirty or more, it is impossible to give beginning readers and writers the individual attention they need. Therefore, the traditional policy on teacher-pupil ratios in primary and secondary schools should be reversed so that the younger the pupils the smaller their classes.

My most recent research with fifty reception class children in a virtually EPA school has also convinced me that teachers of new school entrants should not only have less than twenty pupils but a 'staggered' intake and a qualified helper of nursery assistant status. This would allow them to spend time really getting to know their pupils' abilities and interests in order to structure appropriate language-learning situations for them.

Open-plan schools
Second, research (my own included) shows a close association between poor reading standards and poor primary school buildings. For this reason alone, the Government's primary improvement programmes are to be applauded. Nevertheless, the current trend to replace and remodel schools on open-plan lines is creating problems largely because teachers have not been trained to work in them.

Research evidence to support this trend is lacking. Consequently, it is difficult to refute the charge that the noise and other distractions in some open-plan schools are impeding children's progress towards oracy and literacy.

Expenditure on books
Third, the Government does not control expenditure on books. This has given rise to an unsatisfactory situation in which the book allowance per head, according to the White Paper, 'whilst varying considerably among authorities, has on average been below what is recommended by the Association of Education Committees as necessary to achieve a good standard of provision'.

To promote initial literacy it is essential that teachers are provided with a good supply of books and other resource materials. Clearly many of them are handicapped in this respect. So, it would seem necessary to make it 'unlawful' for local education authorities to fall below a nationally-agreed minimum expenditure on books.

Staff changes
Besides unsatisfactory working conditions, there are other problems which mitigate against children making a successful start with reading and writing. For example, there is an unusually high turnover of infant school staff, especially in inner cities. This can be disastrous at a stage when children particularly need stable relationships with teachers who have a continuing interest in their progress.

The problem of ensuring progress can be partially solved by having a school programme for language development which can be followed by new teachers and tailored to individual needs. However, in suggesting that all schools should have such a programme in any case, one comes across another potential problem. That is, the traditional freedom of British teachers to decide the manner and content of their teaching.

The task itself
Obviously, this freedom makes it crucially important to have preservice courses which clarify what is the most complex problem of all, namely, the nature of the task itself.

Whatever their mother tongue, children find it relatively more difficult to master its written language. There are many obvious reasons for this including the greater formality of written language and the less dramatic clues to meaning it presents.

In English, there is a wider gulf between speech and print than in other alphabetic writing systems. For, twenty-six letters (graphemes) are used to represent forty-four speech sounds (phonemes) or thereabouts depending on the pronunciation considered.

This degree of mismatch is partly due to the 'borrowing' of words from other languages which are generally more difficult than English at the grammatical level because, for example, they have more inflected forms. However, this is no solace to teachers of young children when helping them to cope with the irregularities of phoneme-grapheme correspondence found in commonly-used words such as 'You have heard read'.

Controversial issues
What are teachers to do in these circumstances? Should they join the minority pressing for a total reform of English spelling?

In view of the infinitely greater cost and upheaval of such a revolutionary measure compared with the recent decimalization and forthcoming metrication, surely they must be realistic. Either they decide to continue teaching traditional orthography from the beginning, or they settle for one of the approaches which 'regularize' the writing system for beginners. Of course, whatever their choice of medium they will be faced with decisions about methods and materials.

Regularized writing systems
Of the regularized systems, the initial teaching alphabet has received the most attention from research workers and the mass media. It is also the

only one so far to be the subject of inquiries sponsored by the Schools Council (Warburton and Southgate 1969). Soon, however, materials will be available in another medium involving minimal spelling changes i.e. *Regularized Inglish* (Wijk 1973).

Teachers who prefer a possible solution which retains conventional spelling may choose a colour-coding system of which the best known are *Words in Colour* (Gattegno 1962) and *Colour Story Reading* (Jones 1967). They might also be interested in using diacritical marking systems such as those devised by Fry (1964) and by Johnson (1972).

Methods
Although inventors of writing systems, authors of schemes and miscellaneous experts give advice on methods, teachers have to make the decisions, and this can be hard on new recruits. If they choose whole-word methods to begin with they should realize the limitations of picture, configuration and context clues for developing independence in word attack. In other words, they must not delay too long the introduction of phonic and structural analysis and eventually dictionary usage.

The advantages and disadvantages of language-experience approaches must also be recognized. For instance, these approaches give children an insight into some purposes of written language and its relationship to spoken language. But they do not intrinsically provide for systematic progression towards an understanding of phoneme-grapheme correspondence, which is essential for reading and spelling. Moreover, teachers who encourage children to compose their own words and sentences using the apparatus of *Breakthrough to Literacy* (Mackay *et al* 1970), should be consciously aware that learning to write reinforces the learning to read process.

Those who operate an integrated day can make reading and writing meaningful activities within a complex of interesting, learning experiences. However, unless one is a good organizer and has a diagnostic, systematic approach for each child with clear objectives and plenty of practice in mind, progress towards literacy will be impeded.

As for team teaching, this obviously requires a consensus of opinion about aims and how they are to be executed. The most experienced teachers can assist the children whose needs are greatest. But the whole operation has to be carefully planned to make the best use of available teaching power and resource materials. Here, of course, it is comparatively easy to use television and other audio-visual aids for developing oracy and literacy.

Materials
When it comes to choosing materials, as already indicated teachers are not equally fortunate. However, assuming that allowances are adequate, they can readily stock library corners for there are plenty of lovely books for children to look at and have read to them.

Meanwhile, teachers who feel the need for basal schemes are not so

well-served. Among other things, those available are not sufficiently comprehensive or structured in the various, necessary ways to promote true independence in reading and writing. Hence, experienced, knowledgeable teachers try to combine several schemes into one programme, nonetheless aware that this forced union is far from satisfactory because the contributory schemes reflect different philosophies, types of experience, knowledge and so on.

Clearly, the kind of foundation scheme which would give busy teachers and young learners the support they need must have a total-language, multisensory approach to literacy, and be so structured as to be a diagnostic instrument in itself. Besides being attractive in content, style, illustration and format, it must also be firmly based on knowledge culled from relevant disciplines as well as being flexible in use. This means that it has to be the product of a multidisciplinary team which includes creative writers and artists all working together with publishing personnel right from the start. In short, it must be different in conception and execution from British schemes already published by August, 1973.

Final word

Because of space restrictions, much has had to be left out of this discussion such as the current controversy about alphabet names, capitalization and punctuation. Perhaps most important of all, what constitutes a sound foundation for literacy has been merely implied by the choice of topics and terms like 'sound' with its double-edged meaning. Therefore, as a final word, a brief indication of my views on this topic would seem appropriate.

When children begin the middle years of schooling, those who already have a sound foundation for literacy can understand standard English and express themselves clearly in the school situation. They are consciously aware of the manifold purposes of written language and its main relationships to and differences from the spoken language. They can sight-read and critically appraise library books suitable for their age, not merely regurgitate the last book of a basal series learned by heart. They are able to recognize and write the common, 'irregular' structure words as well as those containing the major spelling patterns of English. They can write simple prose in narrative form without a teacher's aid, and readily use appropriate dictionary and other reference sources. What is more, they enjoy all these activities, and confidently look forward to the next stages on the road to becoming fully literate.

References

BEREITER, C. and ENGLEMANN, S. (1966) *Teaching Disadvantaged Children in Preschool* New Jersey: Prentice Hall

COULTHARD, M. (1969) A discussion of restricted and elaborated codes *Educational Review* 22, 1, 38-50

DEUTSCH, M. P. (1963) 'The disadvantaged child and the learning process' in H. Passow (Ed) *Education in Depressed Areas* Columbia, New York: Teachers College Press

DUNN, L. and SMITH, O. (1967) *The Peabody Language Development Kits* Minneapolis, Minn.: American Guidance Services

FRY, E. (1964) 'The diacritical marking system and a preliminary comparison with ita' in J. Downing and A. L. Brown (Eds) *The Second International Symposium* London: Cassell

GATTEGNO, C. (1962) *Words in Colour* Reading: Educational Explorers

JOHNSON, H., JONES, D. R., COLE, A. C. and WALTERS, M. B. (1972) The use of diacritical marks in teaching beginners to read *British Journal of Educational Psychology* 42, 2, 120-126

JONES, J. K. (1967) *Colour Story Reading* London: Nelson

MACKAY, D., THOMPSON, B. and SCHAUB, P. (1970) *Breakthrough to Literacy* London: Longman

MORRIS, J. M. (1966) *Standards and Progress in Reading* Slough: NFER

MORRIS, J. M. (1972) 'From speech to print and back again' in V. Southgate (Ed) *Literacy at All Levels* London: Ward Lock Educational

MORRIS, J. M. (1973) 'You can't teach what you don't know' in M. Clark and A. Milne (Eds) *Reading and Related Skills* London: Ward Lock Educational

ROSEN, H. (1972) *Language and Class: A Critical Look at the Theories of Basil Bernstein* Bristol: The Falling Wall Press

TAYLOR, P. H., EXON, G. and HOLLEY, B. (1972) *A Study of Nursery Education* (Schools Council Working Paper 41) London: Evans/Methuen

THOMAS, V. (1973) Children's use of language in the nursery *Educational Research* 15, 3, 209-216

WARBURTON, F. W. and SOUTHGATE, V. (1969) *ita An Independent Evaluation* (The report of a study carried out for the Schools Council) Edinburgh and London: W and R Chambers and John Murray

WIJK, A. M. (1973) 'How to teach reading by the aid of Regularized Inglish' in M. Clark and A. Milne (Eds) *Reading and Related Skills* London: Ward Lock Educational

6 The appraisal of reading readiness

Derek Thackray

Definitions

Before looking at the meaning of the term 'reading readiness', let us first look at the terms 'reading' and 'readiness'.

The term 'readiness' for any kind of learning refers to the stage when first, the child can learn easily and without emotional strain, and second, the child can learn profitably, in that efforts at teaching give gratifying—or at least satisfactory—results.

Definitions of the term 'reading' are many and often contrasting, as the following definitions instanced by Latham (1968) show:

> Reading involves nothing more than the correlation of a sound image with its corresponding visual image . . . . (Bloomfield and Barnhart 1961)

> Reading is the art of reconstructing from the printed page, the writer's ideas, feelings, moods and sensory impressions. (Artley 1961)

The first definition is very limited; the second very complete. The first is more appropriate for the beginning stage of reading; the second for the adult level. These definitions can be said to mark the beginning and end of a sequential process in the development of reading ability.

Even at the early stages most educationists agree that reading includes more than the ability to recognize and pronounce the words on a page, and would agree that it includes gaining meaning from the printed symbol. A simple definition of 'reading' at the beginning stages would be the recognition and understanding of printed words and sentences.

Bearing in mind our definition of 'readiness' and 'reading', reading readiness has been defined by Downing and Thackray (1971) as 'the stage in the child's development when, either through maturation or through previous learning, or both, the individual child can learn to read easily and profitably'. There are many abilities, skills, influences and interests which may develop through maturation or learning and thereby contribute in some measure to the stage of readiness for beginning to learn to read. However, a long list of specific traits and influences that determine a child's readiness for reading would not be particularly helpful to the busy teacher who is rightly more concerned to know *which* abilities and skills are the most important ones. Armed with this kind of knowledge the prereading activities she organizes will be both purposeful and effective in getting her children ready for reading.

A very careful study of the research literature and a rigorous analysis of all the factors contributing to reading readiness shows that the most important ones are general intellectual ability, vocabulary and concept development, auditory discrimination, visual discrimination, the ability to pay attention and follow directions, and left to right orientation. Bearing in mind these important reading readiness factors, how do we know when a child is ready for reading? This is not an easy task but when classes are large in number, any help the teacher can be given in her task of appraising reading readiness is valuable; in such appraisal it is necessary to consider the many and varied items which contribute to readiness.

Methods of appraising reading readiness

The three main methods by which teachers in many American schools gather information concerning readiness are:

1 the direct observation of each child's behaviour
2 the use of an intelligence test
3 the use of a reading readiness test.

Direct observation of children's behaviour

Teachers' judgments regarding a child's readiness for reading have been shown to be very sound. The reasons for this are likely to be complex, but obviously a teacher who gets to know her pupils personally soon becomes sensitive to each individual's development in a wide range of aspects of growth—a much wider range than is sampled by either reading readiness tests or tests of general intelligence.

In experiments, where teachers' judgments have been valid, the teachers have used a reading readiness inventory of some kind. A number of reading readiness inventories have been produced in America, for example Lamoreaux and Lee (1943), Betts (1946), Russell (1949), Harris (1961) and Gray (1956). In this country Schonell (1961) produced a reading readiness chart, and very recently Downing and Thackray (1971) have suggested a reading readiness inventory for consideration by British teachers. These inventories usually cover all the main factors in reading readiness, for example, physiological factors, environmental factors and intellectual factors. Teachers in this country on the whole prefer to keep their own records on children's development towards readiness for reading, and according to Morris (1958) judge reading readiness more by 'instinct' than by a structured means of appraisal. However Goodacre (1967) reported on characteristics of development as signs of reading readiness recorded by the headteachers from one hundred infant departments and schools. In this report we have a clearer picture of the ways in which teachers judge the reading readiness of their children, and it is interesting to note the importance they attach to children's attitudes to reading activities—such as interest in books, interest in print, interest in stories—as compared with perceptual, language, environmental and intellectual considerations.

Intelligence tests
Since general intelligence is an important factor in readiness for reading, and since many investigations have indicated that a certain minimum mental age is necessary for success in reading, group or individual intelligence tests are often used in American schools for appraising readiness for reading. Schonell (1961) wrote that for the appraisal of reading readiness with British children, too, mental age is useful. He recommends as possible individual tests the Stanford-Binet Intelligence Scale (Terman and Merrill 1955), and as a group test the Moray House Picture Intelligence Test (Mellone 1944). The recommendations are not realistic, however, as British teachers are not permitted to use either the Stanford-Binet test or the Wechsler Intelligence Scale for Children, and in my experience the Moray House Picture Intelligence Test is too difficult for children below the age of six. The only suitable one, sometimes used, is the Goodenough Draw-a-Man Test. However, as the minimum mental age hypothesis is no longer tenable, this method can no longer be supported.

Reading readiness tests
Since 1930 in America reading readiness tests have become more numerous and are now quitely widely used there. These tests are usually group tests consisting of a number of subtests of the pencil and paper kind; they are similar to intelligence tests but they differ in that they are directed specifically at skills which the research literature shows are connected with reading. Standish (1959) analysed eight American reading readiness tests and found that, of the eight, all use a test of visual discrimination, six use tests of vocabulary, three use motor tests, two use tests of the reproduction of patterns and shapes from memory, and two make use of tests of relationship. Other tests used include: ability to recall a story, ability to remember ideas in sequence, pronunciation, rhyming of words, auditory discrimination, and handedness and eyedness.

The most widely used reading readiness tests in America are the Gates Reading Readiness Test (Gates 1939), the Harrison Stroud Reading Readiness Profiles (Harrison and Stroud 1956), the Metropolitan Readiness Tests (Hildreth and Griffiths 1948) and the Monroe Reading Aptitude Tests (Monroe 1935). In addition to general reading readiness tests there are a number of tests used in America which are connected with a basic reading series; these tests are composed of subtests and some items relate to the material to be found in the basic readers.

Gates, Bond and Russell (1939), Betts (1948) and Harrison and Stroud (1956) have emphasized the diagnostic value of reading readiness tests. Betts feels that these tests have been a potent factor in further interest in reading readiness problems. He argues that, first, they make it possible for the teacher to identify specific strengths and weaknesses in certain areas, such as visual and auditory discrimination, background of information, vocabulary, perception of relationships; and second, that the fairly specific nature of the tests makes it possible to suggest relevant procedure for developing reading readiness subskills.

There are no British reading readiness tests, but I standardized the first British Reading Readiness Test in 1973 and will now give a brief description of them.

The Thackray Reading Readiness Profiles

The Thackray Reading Readiness Profiles were designed to provide the busy teacher with a quick, convenient and reliable measure of the most important reading readiness factors. Once the teacher knows her children's strengths and weaknesses in these vital reading readiness skills and abilities, she can take positive steps to develop these skills and abilities in her children. My view is that the teacher must not await the stage of reading readiness but must actively bring each child to this stage by developing in them the necessary skills and abilities. It is even more important for the teacher to develop readiness in children from poor home backgrounds in this way, as there is growing research evidence to show that children from such backgrounds are, at the age of seven, well below average reading standards and are often permanently educationally disadvantaged because of this.

The Thackray Reading Readiness Profiles have not been designed to tell a teacher when a child is or is not ready for reading. It would be unrealistic to do this in a short battery of tests when one considers the very many maturational and environmental influences affecting readiness for reading, some of which are outside the teacher's control. Even so, the results will indicate quite clearly those children who are strong in all the reading readiness measures, and who could learn to read with success at once, and also those children who are weak in all the measures and who must not be hurried into learning to read. However, for the majority of children the profiles aim to be diagnostic and to provide the teacher with valuable information about her children's reading readiness activities. Such information can be used by her to provide a stimulating programme of pre-reading activities which include those specific skills and abilities which are so important for learning to read easily and profitably.

The profiles measure directly or indirectly the most important skills and abilities contributing to readiness for reading. They consist of three group measures and one individual measure which are identified as follows:

Profile 1   Vocabulary and concept development
Profile 2   Auditory discrimination
Profile 3   Visual discrimination
Profile 4   General ability

The four abilities mentioned above are measured directly, but in order to complete the measures satisfactorily, a child must pay attention and follow directions, and examine the pictures and words in a left to right sequence so these two abilities are also measured indirectly in the profiles.

Profile 1 Vocabulary and concept development
A key factor affecting the child's state of reading readiness is the background and the cultural level of his home. The effect of home background is revealed in the child's language patterns and speech, knowledge of word meanings and his understanding of basic concepts. This first profile is a measure of the child's vocabulary and concept development, and the words used as test items are objects, actions and concepts within the young child's experience, and are drawn from word lists based on children's early vocabularies. The child selects from the pictures the one that illustrates the word the tester gives. There are twenty-five items, two of which are practice items. Scores are obtained from twenty-three items. The profile takes about fifteen minutes to administer. Below is a test item from the Vocabulary Profile with the appropriate instructions.

(Item 4 Pictures of a screw, a nail, a hook and a drawing pin.) Look at the picture in the pink box at the top of the page. Draw a line under the screw (pause) screw.

Profile 2 Auditory discrimination
Research has shown quite clearly that for learning to read successfully the ability to make auditory discriminations is of vital importance. If a child is not aware that two sounds are the same or different then he cannot understand why words are spelled as they are. Although at first he may acquire a small sight vocabulary, without this ability he will quickly become confused when words look alike, and will be slow to respond to phonic training involving the blending of sounds. This profile measures the child's ability to discriminate between words which do or do not begin with the same initial consonant. The most common initial consonants are used and in addition the three diagraphs 'sh', 'ch' and 'th' (as in *th*ree) which stand for single sounds. As in the Vocabulary Profile the objects illustrated are those familiar to children and drawn from current word lists. There are twenty items of which three are practice items. Scores are obtained from seventeen items. The profile takes about twenty minutes to administer. Below is a test item from the Auditory Discrimination Profile with the appropriate instructions.

(Item 7 Pictures of a window, a table, a lid and a wall.) Look at the pictures in the pink box at the bottom of the page. There is a *w*indow, a *t*able, a *l*id and a *w*all. Draw a line under the *w*indow in the little pink box. Now draw a line under the picture in the long pink box which begins like *w*indow.

Profile 3 Visual discrimination
Again research has shown that a vital skill required for learning to read successfully is that of making accurate visual discriminations when comparing words and letters. This ability is needed in the initial stages of learning to read to build up a sight vocabulary, and later to develop quick

recognition of words for more fluent reading. As in the first two profiles the words used are drawn from word lists based on young children's vocabularies and include words commonly confused visually such as 'house' and 'horse', 'no' and 'on', 'saw' and 'was'. There are thirty-five items, of which three are practice items. Scores are obtained from thirty-two items. The profile takes about fifteen minutes to administer. Below is a test item from the Visual Discrimination Profile with the appropriate instructions.

(Item 2 The words 'saw' 'was' 'sow' and 'sew'.) Look at the words in the next pink box. Draw a line under the word in the little pink box. Now draw a line under the word in the long pink box that is the same as the word in the little pink box.

Profile 4 General ability
This profile is an individual measure of the child's general intellectual ability. The child's skill in drawing his mother and the details he includes, indicates the stage the child has reached in perception and motor control and provides a good estimate of intellectual ability. It is adapted from the Harris (1963) revision of the Goodenough Draw-a-Man Test in which three drawings are completed, and points are allocated for the various parts of the body included in the drawing. However, the norms given are based on the drawings of American children. In this simple adaptation for British children, the child is asked to draw one picture of his or her 'Mummy', as both young boys and girls identify very closely with their mothers. The teacher rates each child's drawing on a five-point scale representing five broad categories of mental development of British children. To enable teachers to make the correct ratings examples of drawings for each of the five categories are provided together with simple verbal notes. The profile takes about ten minutes to administer.

Regarding the interpretation of scores, each raw score on the first three profiles can be converted by consulting the appropriate table in the manual, to a rating of A, B, C, D or E; in the fourth profile each child's drawing is compared with the examples and verbal notes for each rating (A to E) are given in the manual and rated by the teacher. As well as giving complete information on the interpretation of the scores on the profiles, the manual includes details of standardization, and activities the teacher can use to develop her children's language, and visual and auditory discrimination skills.

A reexamination of the concept of reading readiness
In very recent years, both in America and in this country, the validity of the concept of reading readiness has been questioned. Educationists are becoming uncertain and teachers are becoming confused. For example, Lynn (1963) writes '. . . it seems doubtful whether the concept of reading readiness has sufficient substance to be worth retaining' and primary teachers are wondering if they should now ignore reading readiness.

There is certainly need for a new approach to reading readiness, but there is also a danger of putting back the educational clock if a balanced view of recent findings on this subject is not presented. The new approach should not discard the concept but recognize that there can be no decisive answer to the question 'When is a child ready for reading?' because there is no single criterion that applies to all children. The question which should be asked is 'When is *this* particular child ready for *this* particular programme?' as there are two forces affecting the moment of readiness for the child. We can fit the child for reading by developing in him the important reading readiness skills, and we can also fit reading to the child by using simple approaches in media and materials.

Downing (1963) has written, 'The concept of reading readiness does have value and should be retained, provided that the role of learning in development towards readiness is given greater recognition.' I would subscribe to this view, that we must not await readiness but develop it. And if we are to develop reading readiness, we must start with a profile of the child's strengths and weaknesses in the important reading readiness skills.

If the concept of reading readiness were abandoned or minimized, the tendency would be to start all children on formal reading very soon after they entered school. Many children on entering reception classes are nearer four mentally, experientially and emotionally, and they are not ready to read. Hence if individual differences were ignored, many of our children would become failures from the start.

References

ARTLEY, A. S. (1961) *What is Reading?* Chicago: Scott Foresman

BETTS, E. A. (1946) *Foundations of Reading Instruction* New York: American Book

BETTS, E. A. (1948) Remedial and corrective reading: content area approach *Education* 68, 579-96

BLOOMFIELD, L. and BARNHART, C. L. (1961) *Let's Read: a Linguistic Approach* Detroit: Wayne State University

DOWNING, J. and THACKRAY, D. V. (1971) *Reading Readiness* London: University of London Press

GATES, A. I. (1939) *Gates Reading Readiness Tests* Columbia, New York: Teachers' College Press

GATES, A. I., BOND, G. L. and RUSSELL, D. H. (1939) *Methods of Determining Reading Readiness* Columbia, New York: Teachers' College Press

GOODACRE, E. (1967) *Reading in Infant Classes* Slough: NFER

GRAY, W. S. (1956) *Teaching of Reading and Writing: An International Survey* Paris: UNESCO and London: Evans

HARRIS, A. J. (1961) *How to Increase Reading Ability* New York: Longmans Green

HARRIS, D. B. (1963) *Children's Drawings as Measures of Intellectual Maturity* New York: Harcourt, Brace and World

HARRISON, M. L. and STROUD, J. B. (1956) *Harrison-Stroud Reading Readiness Profiles* New York: Houghton Mifflin

HILDRETH, G. M. and GRIFFITHS, N. L. (1948) *Metropolitan Readiness Tests* Yonkers, New York: World Book

LAMOREAUX, L. A. and LEE, D. M. (1943) *Learning to Read through Experience* New York: Appleton-Century-Crofts

LATHAM, W. (1968) 'Are today's teachers adequately trained for the teaching of reading?' in J. Downing and A. L. Brown (Eds) *The Third International Reading Symposium* London: Cassell

LYNN, R. (1963) Reading readiness and the perceptual abilities of young children *Educational Research* 6, 10-15

MELLONE, M. A. (1944) *Moray House Picture Intelligence Test* London: University of London Press

MONROE, M. (1935) *Monroe Reading Aptitude Tests* New York: Houghton-Mifflin

MORRIS, J. M. (1958) *Reading in the Primary School* London: Newnes

RUSSELL, D. H. (1949) *Children Learn to Read* Boston: Ginn

SCHONELL, F. J. (1961) *The Psychology and Teaching of Reading* Edinburgh: Oliver and Boyd

STANDISH, E. J. (1959) Readiness to read *Educational Research* 12, 29-38

TERMAN, L. M. and MERRILL, M. (1961) *Stanford-Binet Intelligence Scale* London: Harrap

WECHSLER, D. (1955) *Wechsler Intelligence Scale for Children* New York: Psychological Corporation

7 British research and beginning reading

Elizabeth Goodacre

Some recent statements about reading research

We should remember that no aspect of the curriculum has had so much money in research and development spent on it as reading. To put it crudely, no aspect of primary school children's activity keeps so many people in lucrative occupations. No one can suggest that beginning reading has been neglected. Can the same be said of primary school children's talk? Or play? Or environmental studies? Or, indeed, their development as autonomous readers?

(Page 270 of Notes on Chapter 4, Item 1, in *The Language of Primary School Children* by Connie and Harold Rosen, Penguin (Schools Council Project).

Two surveys, under the auspices of the Schools Council are due to begin this year. (Vera Southgate at Manchester, E. A. Lunzer at Nottingham) . . . More than twenty other research programmes are being conducted over the United Kingdom—including one at University College, London, into the authorship of educational and school library books and the problems of incorporating the results of reading research.

Page 645 of *New Society* (22nd March, 1973) article in Society at Work series, 'Now read on' by Paul Medlicott, Educational Correspondent.

Also under the Schools Council banner, Vera Southgate is carrying out a survey of Manchester children from seven to nine years old and assessing their working procedures against a framework of all the skills which are used in effective reading: here the concentration will be on remedial techniques. And in Nottingham, E. A. Lunzer is looking at the ten to fourteens, and particularly at their difficulties in moving from primary to secondary schools. In fact, more than twenty other reading research programmes are now going on throughout the country, including one on the problems of coordinating the results of reading research programmes.

(The leader titled 'A good read?' of *Teachers World,* 30th March, 1973).

Who does reading research?
Reading research can be carried out by national organizations such as the National Foundation for Educational Research (NFER), Department of Education and Science (DES), Schools Council, or Social Science Research Council (SSRC), or national associations such as the National Association for Remedial Education (NARE), National Association for Teachers of English (NATE); by LEA remedial or school psychological services or research and statistics groups; or by individuals studying in universities or colleges of education, or study groups organized by teachers centres.

Research in universities
At the present time, higher degree students can carry out reading research within the faculty departments of English, social or educational psychology at different universities, and diploma students in university institutes and B.Ed. students in colleges of education may in certain circumstances offer theses on reading research as part of their work. There is, however, no higher degree course in reading in this country.

Professor Downing (1973), in his comparative study of teaching reading in fourteen different countries, commented on the fact that generally in educational systems, the teachers of the younger children had 'lower' status in the educational pecking order and that university work is considered as 'higher education'. Since most universities do not have courses in 'reading', this gives the impression that reading cannot have 'high status'. He has pointed out the effects of this attitude in relation to the training of teachers, where 'reading' can be neglected because of its 'poor' academic status in relation to other curriculum subjects. Downing reported that the United States was the chief exception—American universities consider reading a proper subject for academic study. Noticeably, reading was also accorded higher 'status' at the 'lower' levels of that country's educational system.

The second and third statements at the beginning of this paper would suggest however that there are a number of research 'programmes' being conducted at the university or national level, and that work is now under way on the problems of coordinating research and, presumably, disseminating the results.

The extent of research 'programmes'
There is in fact no central institution in this country responsible for guiding, coordinating and disseminating the results of investigations and experiments in teaching reading. There is no register of research projects. It is only in the last two years that it has been possible to establish an annual review of published reading research in Britain (Goodacre 1973). The study at University College was *not* into the problems of coordinating results.

To try and find out more about the extent and scope of research 'programmes' at this level, I checked Paul Medlicott's reference for his statement—the volumes of the DES/HMSO publication *Scientific Research in*

British Universities and Colleges and the NFER's *Current Researches in Education and Educational Psychology* for the period 1967-72. For 1971-72, there were indeed some twenty studies listed under the headings 'reading', 'reading aids', 'reading disorders', 'programmes' and 'research', but in several instances the same study was quoted under several headings and some studies were listed throughout the whole period (i.e. ongoing for more than four years). It was possible to list for the *five year period* some forty-eight studies, but this also included consulting the funding records of the SSRC and projects carried out by the NFER and the ILEA Research and Statistics Group.

A letter asking for information about these studies was sent out to the investigator listed for each study, and it is hoped that the resulting information from this 'survey' will enable a register of research to be compiled. The HMSO records etc may be incomplete as a source of information, as I found that none of the studies carried out by the London University Institute of Education MA 'Psychology of Literacy' students were listed, although MA and MEd. students of other universities were listed.

Research at other levels

Reading research is also sometimes carried out as part of the work of the School Psychological Service. In a survey of LEAs in 1970 (Goodacre 1971), some twenty LEAs referred to reading studies or investigations being undertaken as part of the work of this service. These studies tended to be either investigations into the effectiveness of particular reading materials (e.g. SRA *Reading Laboratories, Breakthrough to Literacy* etc) or reading attainment surveys providing information about reading standards and the incidence of reading backwardness. The resulting data was in some cases examined for the effects of factors such as social background, school size, length of infant schooling etc.

A survey of 246 teachers centres (Goodacre in press) asked about local research (e.g. study groups, research projects etc). Comments from some forty centres were recorded, of which fifteen referred to surveys by school or remedial services, five to studies in local colleges of education, and two to study groups connected with NATE projects. Three centres mentioned followup or developmental studies using the Schools Council *Breakthrough* material. Only eight mentioned reading study groups or English working parties which were meeting to discuss and work out small-scale research studies; these were mainly concerned with evaluation of materials and the use of audio visual aids.

Funding of research projects

Table 1 (page 58) lists the projects financed by the Schools Council (in English), DES and SED, and SSRC. It should be noticed that the Schools Council's projects vary in the contribution they make to reading research; e.g. the *Linguistics and English Teaching: Initial Literacy Project* produced the *Breakthrough* material and made available to teachers linguistic information about the relationship between speech, writing and reading. *Written*

Language of 11-18 Year Olds is far less related to the teaching of reading. It has lead, however, to a separate three-year development project *Writing across the Curriculum 11-13*, which is to disseminate the research findings of *Written Language of 11-18 Year Olds* and to study the effects of these findings being put into practice. *Breakthrough* is being evaluated by Jessie Reid (University of Edinburgh—study begun 1969, report due from Longmans 1973), but presumably this investigation was funded out of the *Linguistics and English Teaching: Initial Literacy Project.*

Studying the funding of research programmes by the Schools Council it is clear that priority is now being given to the later stages of reading development, which may give the impression that 'sufficient' attention has been given to the beginning stages.

Table 1

Schools Council Projects	Location	Duration	Cost £
Preschool Language (2-5) R	Leeds Un.	1971-72	8 000
Linguistics and English Teaching: Initial Literacy Project (5-7) T/P	University Coll. Lon.	1964-71	156 700†
ita: An Independent Evaluation (5-8) R*	Manchester Un.	1965-68	3 600
English for Immigrant Children (8-16) T/P/R	Leeds Un.	1966-71	135 250
Review of Postwar Research and Experiments in Method of Teaching Reading (13-18) R	Inst. of Ed., Lon. Un.	1967-70	2 600
Children as Readers (7-18) R	Bristol Un.	1968-73	16 309
Language Development in the Primary School (10-11) R	Inst. of Ed., Lon. Un.	1969-71	11 500
Teaching English to West Indian Children (7-9) T/P/R*	Birmingham Un.	1967-73	55 000
Extending Beginning Reading (7-9) R	Manchester Un.	1973-76	36 300
Question and Response by Children in School (12-16) R	Southampton Un.	1968-73	20 706
English in the Middle Years of Schooling (12-13) R	Goldsmiths' Col. Lon.	1970-72	18 000
Children's Reading Habits (12-16) R	Sheffield Un.	1969-73	21 000
Effective Use of Reading (12-14) R	Nottingham Un.	1973-76	33 000

Table 1—continued

Linguistics and English Teaching: Language in Use (15½-18) T/R*	University Coll. Lon.	1964-71	156	700†
Written Language of 11-18 Year Olds (14-18) R	Inst. of Ed., Lon. Un.	1966-71	33	517
Oracy (11½-18) R	Birmingham Un.	1967-72	16	000
Writing Across the Curriculum (11-13) T	Inst. of Ed., Lon. Un.	1971-74	31	000

DES/SED Projects

Factors influencing Early Progress in Reading	Strathclyde Un.	1969-71		—
ita: First and Second Experiments (10½-12) R	Inst. of Ed., Lon.	1964-67	3	500
		1962-64	9	500
Colour Story Reading R	Inst. of Ed., Lon.	1965-67	1	600
Teaching Reading to Deaf Children (10-14)	Manchester Un.	1967-71	21	000
Reading Disability R	Strathclyde Un.	1966-68	4	500
Reading Survey in England and Wales R	Nat. Found. Ed. Res.	1970-72		—

SSRG Projects

Standardization of a Reading Test	St. Paul's Coll. of Ed.	1972-74	1	740
Further Statistical Analysis of ita Data	Inst. of Ed., Lon.	1967-68	3	476
Further Development of Techniques for Studying and Influencing Reading as a Learning Skill	Brunel Un.	1970-72	16	293
Psycholinguistic Study of Comprehension in Reading (13-18)	Dundee Un.	1971-73	80	565
Teaching Machine Project (10-18)	Newcastle Un.	1968-70	8	957
Cognitive Process and Educational Attainment of Socially Handicapped Children (17-18)	University Coll. Lon.	1971-73	4	996
Auditory-visual Matching in Retarded Readers (14-15)	Manchester Un.	1971-73	3	794
Teaching of Reading in Scottish Primary and Secondary Schools	Queen Margaret Coll.	1972-76	83	145

Key: R report; P pupil material; T teacher material; *some or all materials published 31st March, 1972; T received funds in addition to Schools Council.

Funding for beginning reading

The Linguistics and English Teaching Project received a total of £156,000, including the contribution made by the Nuffield Programme, and this amount was used for both the *Initial Literacy* and *Language in Use* (11-18+ pupils) studies. The other six projects related directly to reading came to approximately £111,000 and two of these projects accounting for £69,000 were funded only recently (1973-76) and are for the later stages of reading development. The other three projects (a review of methods research, the ita evaluation and the NATE *Children as Readers* project) are those most concerned with the beginning stages, and have received funds of £23,500.

Possibly the other beginning reading studies which are most familiar to teachers are the ita experiments. It should be remembered that the Ford Foundation and the DES largely financed this research; the contribution of the latter was £13,000. As Philip and Goyen (1973) pointed out in their survey of British reading innovations, Jones' *Colour Story Reading* was the only other signalling innovation to receive financial support for experimental investigation (£1,600).

It would seem that the most financial support on a national basis has been given to examining the contribution of linguistics to the teaching of reading and the development of the *Breakthrough* material, and on a smaller scale, investigation and evaluation of the contribution of 'signalling' devices at the beginning stages. If then it is agreed that valuable as this research has been, there is room for more research into the initial stages, where should this be concentrated?

Priorities in beginning reading

In a paper of this length, there is insufficient space to go into this question in great detail, but my own list of preferences would certainly include:

1 Further research into reading attainment measures for young children, including informal methods of recording progress.
2 Further research into the understanding by young children of the terms used in reading instruction, particularly as related to phonic teaching.
3 Further research into children's 'miscues' or oral reading errors to determine whether these are related to stages of cognitive development or can be related to the types of reading material in use.
4 Research into the effectiveness of different methods of reading instruction with boys and with girls.

Readers can probably add to this list and I would be interested to hear from anyone with views on this question of priorities.

Does 'reading' research generally get 'sufficient' funding?

Finally, it could be argued that funds are not available for further research at the beginning stages because the financing of reading research generally is inadequate. Certainly, at this stage it might be useful to consider some of the other projects and their amounts funded by the Schools Council and consider whether 'reading' has had sufficient consideration. Projects funded solely by the Schools Council include:

Project Technology (for five years) £287,000
Education for a Multiracial Society (four years) £136,500
Bilingual Educational Project (seven years) £107,754
Welsh as a First Language at Primary and Secondary Level (five years) £103,000
CSE Monitoring Procedures (five years) £133,556
Research into CSE and 16+ Exam (seven years) £102,100
Modern Languages (ten years) £831,000
Mathematics for the Majority (13-16) and Continuation Programme (eight years) £152,000

Also a number of large national curriculum development projects came to an end last year, and East Anglia University has received £66,000 from Fords to research into the effects of curriculum development projects, i.e. what actually happens in the schools after a project has come to an end. It is hoped that this research will find ways by which the momentum built up by curriculum innovation can be sustained after the official end of a project.

In other words, it is becoming obvious that it is not enough to fund research but finance must also be available for the dissemination of results and the provision of feedback channels of communication. This problem will apply to reading research as much as to any other aspect of curriculum development. As at the moment there are some 114 Schools Council projects in the pipeline, it looks as if what will be important in the next few years is the amount of influence and support afforded to reading research findings in the various localities rather than the level of interest existing among teachers e.g. provision of courses, exhibitions of materials etc at teachers centres; informed and knowledgeable advisers and inspectorate; readable, brief reports or an easily available abstracting service or journal.

References
DOWNING, J. (1973) *Comparative Reading—Crossnational studies of Behaviour and Processes in Reading and Writing* New York: Collier-Macmillan
GOODACRE, E. J. (1971) *Provision for Reading* Reading: School of Education, University of Reading
GOODACRE, E. J. (1973) *Reading Research 1972* Centre for the Teaching of Reading (School of Education, University of Reading), 29 Eastern Avenue, Reading RG1 5RO. The Centre has also produced *Reading Research 1968-72* (1973) and *Reading Research 1971* (1972)
GOODACRE, E. J. (in the press) *Teachers Centres and the Teaching of Reading* Reading: School of Education, University of Reading

PHILIP, H. and GOYEN, J. (1973) *Innovation in Reading in Britain*
UNESCO:IBE Experiments and Innovations in Education No. 3
London: HMSO

Day 2
Convenor: Chris Walker

8 The reading curriculum for the middle years of schooling

John E. Merritt

The printed word still provides us with a system for communicating information in a form that is, in many respects, unsurpassable. It is likely to do so for a very long time to come—for good reason. It is compact—a wealth of information can be packed into a very small space. It is highly portable—a massive amount of information can easily be carried in a pocket or a small brief case. It has no mechanical disadvantages—it requires no power and virtually no maintenance. Information can readily be found—a contents list or index can get you straight to the required page. And it is cheap. The disciples of McLuhan who decry the need for reading are simply ignoring the evidence—the phenomenal increase of printed material that is produced, and read, each year.

The individual who cannot cope with this 'avalanche of print' is seriously disadvantaged in the modern world. And the individual who cannot derive pleasure from reading the printed word must surely be regarded as culturally deprived.

The ability to identify individual words is of course merely one small part of the problem. To cope with print effectively in functional reading we need to be able to define each information need, to locate suitable sources, to select from a wide range of material, to read selectively and purposefully, and to continue to develop the skills required to do all this competently in each information need area. To appreciate literature it is necessary to have a very general knowledge of the treasure-chest available and to be able to relate to a work of literature in a way that permits the essence to be savoured. The development of all these skills and attributes constitutes the goal of the reading curriculum.

There are three sets of considerations to be taken into account in making decisions about the reading curriculum for the middle years of schooling. The first, and the more obvious, is that the reading curriculum should include whatever is necessary to help children to cope with *the reading demands of the general curriculum*. The second is that it should prepare children so that they can cope with *the reading demands of the adult world*. And third, the reading curriculum must also provide for the development of interest in *reading as an activity that is valued for its own sake*.

The reading demands of the general curriculum
It is important to remember that reading is a major activity in learning

about almost every subject in the curriculum. One task in designing a reading curriculum, therefore, is to help children *to learn how to learn through reading*. Another important factor to take into account is the diminished reliance on the single textbook. Instead of merely learning to read a few pages suggested by the teacher, children must now learn how to specify their own reading purposes, how to locate and select suitable reading material for a particular topic or project, how to organize their reading and recording, and how to complete a reading assignment by combining material from different sources in some suitable form. We can think of this as the completion of a *reading cycle* (see Merritt 1973).

Learning how to learn through reading
Almost every study of learning shows that learning is much easier when the learner actively organizes or reorganizes material instead of merely relying on rote learning. But the organization or reorganization of material is precisely what is needed in order to achieve reading comprehension. The achievement of comprehension calls for the organization of factual detail into main ideas, the critical evaluation of what is there, or not there, in terms of these organizing concepts, the drawing of inferences from this meaning structure and so on. Making an effort to achieve the highest level of comprehension, rather than merely trying to rote-learn a text seems, therefore, to be the obvious way to assist later recall.

Unfortunately, many subject teachers do not seem to appreciate this. Instead, they regularly set learning tasks without making any sort of serious or informed effort to encourage pupils to strive for meaning and understanding. Yet without this there is no point in trying to learn the material in the first place.

One way to encourage children to achieve higher levels of comprehension is to set appropriate questions. But if children are using a variety of texts for a variety of reading purposes, it is obviously impossible for the teacher to set all the different kinds of comprehension questions that could be devised to ensure that the reading is thorough. And, of course, this might not be desirable even if it were possible. (This problem is dealt with in some detail by Farnes 1973). After all, children have to learn to think for themselves. It is no good making them dependent on comprehension questions thought up by somebody else.

I would like to suggest two approaches to this problem: one is through *comparative reading* and the other is through *cooperative reading*.

Comparative reading
Getting information about a topic from more than one text provides an obvious incentive to pupils to check facts, note omissions, make inferences, and so on, that is to say, to develop the various comprehension skills. For example, a pupil might get certain impressions about an historical event after reading an English textbook and an entirely different impression after reading, say, a Scottish, American, or French textbook. Almost inevitably, therefore, he would be led to undertake some kind of critical evaluation.

Here, the teacher in middle schools might well seek the help of colleagues in secondary schools. These teachers can get their more able pupils to translate school textbooks obtained from primary schools in France, Germany, or any other country whose language they are learning. These translations can then be read by the younger pupils who can compare them with their own school texts. This is an invaluable exercise for the older pupils as much as for the younger children. Discussion between the two groups about the discrepancies between the English and the translated texts is likely to help to improve the reading of both groups in various aspects of comprehension—as well as throwing some light on certain problems of translation.

The comparative reading of reports in different newspapers provides opportunities for noting other kinds of bias. It provides a positive incentive, therefore, to note whether important factual details are suppressed, how opinion may masquerade as fact, and how appeals to authority are often used as substitutes for evidence. A comparative reading of different biology textbooks might force a child to recognize that there are many different ways of classifying and organizing knowledge. In fact, comparative reading of any kind provides a positive incentive to children to exercise various kinds of comprehension even without the stimulus of predetermined questions. This stimulus can provide a basis for the development of the second approach—cooperative reading.

Cooperative reading
Reading, even for the more able child, can be a rather lonely activity. In comparative reading, however, there is every reason to make the activity a cooperative effort. This can happen quite naturally. When a group of children are working together on some inquiry or project they will sooner or later have to pool the results of their separate reading activities. It is a simple and obvious step for them to discuss some of their problems as they actually work through the different texts. With only a little encouragement from the teacher, they will begin to debate all the various kinds of issue referred to above in the discussion of comparative reading.

There are dangers—of course. They may quarrel and fight over trivial issues, they may show off, they may disparage the reasonable efforts of other children, and they may victimize the pupil who shows any originality. But heaven help us if we merely try to suppress this behaviour. If the children are genuinely motivated their mutual need provides an ideal context for the development of constructive and cooperative activity. And when aggressive signs do reassert themselves—as they will from time to time—the skilled teacher can intervene to harness this aggression by diverting attention back to the text.

This is the point at which the sheer professionalism of the teacher counts—his ability to teach children, not just skills. In fact, the teacher may not even identify the skills he is teaching at the time. *He simply needs to be clear about what the pupils really want to know, and find interesting,* and ask questions which will help them to clarify *their* thinking. This, in itself, requires a great deal of skill. But sheer commonsense and a sensitive regard for the pupils' own purposes can go a very long way. If, on the other hand, the teacher gets obsessed with the idea of making a particular point, or engages in a ruthless inquisition, the children will soon lapse into apathy—or a sullen semblance of cooperation.

Once the teacher has established the pattern of comparative and cooperative reading, the whole process can, and must, become self-generating. Children can soon get into the habit of comparing texts and asking relevant questions of each other. And the more they do this, the more perceptive their questions tend to become. But everything depends upon the quality of the control exercised by the teacher. This is what determines whether or not the children will *learn how to learn* through reading.

Even the most traditional teachers can be remarkably sensitive in their control and their use of questions. And some who would regard themselves as progressive can be surprisingly domineering. Relating to pupils is a matter of professional competence rather than curriculum theory. Given such competence, comparative and cooperative reading provide excellent opportunities for helping children to learn how to learn through reading, even if the teacher is not a specialist in reading. The implication of this is that teachers in every subject area can and must play an important part in helping to provide this part of the reading curriculum.

Reading demands of the adult world

In the conventional curriculum the reading matter which children encounter will be largely restricted to books. The more up to date teacher may introduce a limited amount of additional material—facsimiles of original documents in history, travel brochures in geography, and so on. This material is very limited in range, however, compared with the range of material that adults have to cope with.

In addition, the children's purposes for reading this material may be very different indeed from typical adult purposes—and our purposes affect the skills we need to use. The conventional kinds of curriculum, therefore, provide only a very limited range of experience in terms of the reading demands of the adult world.

This is a serious problem for two reasons. First, children do not have the opportunity to develop all the skills necessary for effective adult reading. Second, and even more important, the kinds of reading habit they do acquire may be hard to overcome. This may prevent many children from ever achieving the levels of competence that a wider range of reading experience might have permitted.

In order to decide what kind of adult reading might sensibly be introduced into the curriculum we must, of course, first look at adult reading in general. We can then decide what might be done to provide a suitable form of preparation in the school years.

Categories of adult reading

The first thing to recognize, and this comes hard to the specialist subject teacher, is that adult reading does not fall conveniently into subject categories such as 'history', 'geography', 'biology', and so on. The categories of adult reading relate much more closely to the kinds of situation which adults have to cope with and the various *roles* they play in each kind of situation. They relate to the kinds of *information needs* they have in each of these role situations.

In deciding which particular role and information need categories to work from, two major considerations are:

1 convenience—do the categories help us to group together materials which are most often needed at the same time?
2 practicality—do these categories provide a simple enough grouping for them to be of practical value, and not merely theoretical interest?

For reasons which I have explained in more detail elsewhere (Merritt 1974), the role categories which seem to me to fit these criteria quite well are as follows:

Roles Home and Family; Employment; Consumer, Leisure; Community.

These categories may be further subdivided in any number of ways—and not necessarily by the teacher. The pupils themselves might be encouraged to decide on their own categories—bearing in mind the two criteria given above. Even so, the teacher needs to have some ideas of his own against which to compare the pupils' choices. And he must be prepared to modify these if the pupils' ideas happen to be better than his own!

In addition to working out these subcategories, the teacher needs to have worked out a whole variety of ways in which any particular project or investigation might go. The following information-need categories provide a useful way of doing this.

Information needs
01 Knowledge of what is necessary for survival, or for achieving reasonably comfortable role conditions:
   1 *Positive:* nutrition, respiration, elimination, warmth.
   2 *Negative:* internal safety (from noxious food, fumes, etc.
                 external safety (from objects, fire, excessive noise etc)

02 Knowledge of how each need or satisfier may be correctly identified:
   1 *Internal:* hunger/s, thirst, muscular tension etc.
   2 *External:* sight, smell, touch, taste, sound.

03 Knowledge of relevant physical actions and techniques for satisfying each need:
   1 *Locomotion:* personal, mechanical transportation.
   2 *Manipulation:* personal skills, tools and machines.

04　Knowledge of others and how to cooperate in ways relevant to the satisfying of each (mutual or complementary) need:
　　1　*Communication:* verbal, written, paralinguistic.
　　2　*Interaction:* leading, following, sharing.

05　Knowledge of how to get knowledge relevant to the satisfaction of needs:
　　1　*Goals:* identification and selection of relevant sources.
　　2　*Plans:* organization for accessing sources.
　　3　*Implementation:* processing information sources.
　　4　*Development:* making full use of knowledge gained about how to get knowledge.

06　Knowledge of how to decide priorities:
　　1　Knowledge of basis of existing preference systems and how they may have developed.
　　2　Knowledge of principles that might reasonably be considered in modifying preferences.
　　3　Knowledge of how to clarify decision problems (e.g. by constructing decision trees, weighting scales etc).

Preparing for adult reading
Now it is quite obvious that the practising teacher cannot possibly be expected to explore *all* the various possibilities for reading in each of these areas before deciding what is worth introducing into the reading curriculum. (I would argue, however, that any course of initial training for teachers which does not cover this kind of ground adequately is palpably deficient in its ordering of priorities.) And, in any case, the content to be studied will tend to change, in some cases quite rapidly, as each year passes.

Fortunately, however, these difficulties can be turned to positive advantage. For instead of having the ability to provide some rigid course which all must follow, the teacher must now learn along with the pupils. And this adoption of a learning role by the teacher may help him to establish, or develop, the ability to accept the pupils' interests as legitimate starting points. Hopefully, he will then concentrate more on the *process* by which they acquire knowledge.

This does not, of course, mean that *content* is to be neglected or regarded as unimportant. On the contrary—this is an unfortunately widespread fallacy. A concentration on the *process* of getting information should in fact result in a vast improvement in *content* also.

In trying to see how all this might work out in practice it is helpful to think of the filing system, or resource unit, that could be developed to cope with the printed material that might be studied in each of these categories. This might look something like the diagram below. Each time a particular project or investigation is started which relates to any of these headings, the printed materials that are gathered can be filed in the appropriate section. As some sections fill up more rapidly than others, the empty or half-empty sections can then provide a continuous challenge, 'What else should we know about that belongs in that area?'

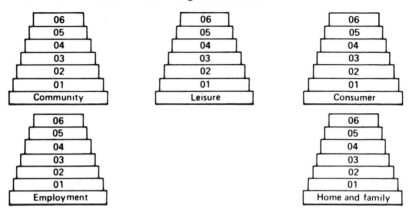

This kind of system provides one way of introducing children to a wide array of adult information needs. This is only part of the problem, however. The questions asked by children, and the material they refer to, are not necessarily the questions and the materials that relate to adult reading. Children's purposes are not the same as adult purposes. Nevertheless, studies that originate solely in the pupils' spontaneous interests often lead into studies that are of more general significance. Each time this happens, the children can be introduced to questions relating to adult purposes as well as their own. Thus the study of pond life may lead to a study of water pollution, and this can be related to other studies in the 01/Home and Family area—or it can be treated as an 01/Community problem.

Again, the environmental study may lead from a review of neighbourhood resources to a study of changes in employment patterns and on to a prediction of job opportunities, i.e. a study relevant to later employment. Each type of job can then be considered in terms of the extent to which the various 01-06 needs are likely to be catered for.

Following this pattern, each role-need area is given a firm basis of general studies and is not merely treated at a superficial level in terms of short-term issues. In addition, the direct study of *the relationships* between general school learning and everyday life problems in this way provides the most appropriate content for helping pupils to see the relevance of both. It provides a context in which the reading is motivated by a variety of purposes and, I suggest, a most appropriate context for developing the ability to cope with adult reading demands. Within this context, the enterprising teacher will always see a variety of ways in which he can further enrich the experience of reading related to adult purposes. He will encourage pupils to prepare and complete questionnaires, to write and read rules, regulations and instructions, to construct adverts, to design notices, and so on. In short, he will introduce the whole range of media that adults are called upon to read into the everyday life of the school (see Moyle, 1973). And, of course, he will encourage cooperative and comparative reading in this context also.

Reading as an activity that is valued for its own sake

A large amount of a child's reading in school is functional reading—reading that is undertaken primarily as a means to some end. For many children this kind of reading is felt to be a rather boring and unrewarding business. And the more of it they do, the less they are inclined to value reading for its own sake. The first task, therefore, is to make the functional reading a pleasurable activity.

If some of the suggestions made in the earlier sections of this paper are followed this task should not be quite so difficult. When children are motivated to read to satisfy their own purposes, the reading itself is that much more acceptable. The cooperative approach, well handled, can make it a positively agreeable activity. For a number of children, this will be sufficient to induce a positive interest in reading for its own sake in a number of the fields of interests they develop. Given this sort of development it is somewhat easier to develop an interest in reading the kind of material that is sometimes classed as 'children's literature'. (The quotation marks indicate a certain reservation about the use of this expression; the reasons for holding such reservations are ably elaborated by Davis 1973.)

There are many occasions, in following the children's own interests, when a poem, a story, or a play, may provide material that is just as valid as that found in the textbook. An historical novel, for example, may sometimes provide a more authentic set of impressions, in some respects, than a history book. A contemporary novel may provide a more valuable set of impressions, in some respects, than a geography book or a political text. Here, comparative reading of the different kinds of source material can lead to fascinating discussions on the nature of evidence and the relative validity and adequacy of different kinds of material.

Relating children's literature to functional reading in this way raises a question that tends to be neglected by the English specialist: does it make sense to think in terms of 'an adequate diet' in terms of the works of literature to which a child is exposed? A limited range of textbooks, or a diet of biased textbooks, may effectively cripple a child's ability to range over the wider intellectual field, or to view certain kinds of issue objectively. Might the same hold good in the case of literature? Should this too cover the whole range of human roles and needs? And should it cover the whole spectrum of humanity instead of being restricted largely to one particular culture? Might it be that the self-selected band of writers of children's books provide books that are good in themselves but which are inadequate in the extent to which they cover the human condition?

To these questions I cannot even offer a tentative answer. But I think that they must be faced by anyone who seeks to provide an adequate reading curriculum.

References

LAYBOURN, M. (1971) Structuring a programme of graded exercises in social literacy for less able pupils *Reading* 5, iii, 14-18

MERRITT, J. E. (1970) Priorities in curriculum design *Durham and Newcastle Institutes of Education Journal* 22, CX, 44-7

MERRITT, J. E. (1974) *What Shall We Teach?* London: Ward Lock Educational

THE OPEN UNIVERSITY (1972) J. E. Merritt for the Curriculum: Context, Design and Development Course Team *Unit 10: A Framework for Curriculum Design* Milton Keynes: The Open University Press

THE OPEN UNIVERSITY (1973) Alan Davis for the Reading Development Course Team *Unit 2: Literature for Children* Milton Keynes: The Open University Press

THE OPEN UNIVERSITY (1973) N. C. Farnes for the Reading Development Course Team *Units 3 and 4: Reading Purposes Comprehension and the Use of Context* Milton Keynes: The Open University Press

THE OPEN UNIVERSITY (1973) J. E. Merritt for the Reading Development Course Team *Unit 1: Perspectives on Reading* Milton Keynes: The Open University Press

9 The significance of visual, ocular and postural anomalies in reading and writing

C. H. Bedwell

Introduction

For some years I have been interested in the clinical problem of discomfort and/or reduction of visual efficiency for near visual tasks, such as reading (Bedwell 1970, 1971, 1972a, 1972b). As a clinician, therefore, I have been interested in learning to observe any anomaly, particularly visual, ocular, and postural, that may be present. In many cases, these are signs and symptoms which could pass unnoticed, yet would enable a better under- standing of, for example, a poorer reading performance than might be expected from the child's intelligence, or why a child has difficulty in reading aloud.

Outline of the research project

The research described is part of a combined study by myself on ocular aspects, Dr C. Binney, of St Bartholomews Hospital, and his colleagues, on neurology, Miss M. Newsome with psychological tests, and Mr G. Raisin, the headmaster of the school.

All the children were examined visually and ocularly, both by conven- tional methods and by special techniques developed by myself. Studies were made of the child's posture, the state of the binocular coordination of the eyes for different directions of gaze, of laterality, and of eye domi- nance for distance and near, using different types of tests, and of sense of order. The light threshold contrasts for each eye were assessed over the central field of vision on the Visual Field Analyser. Investigations were made of eye-movement, both photographically and electronically, while the child was writing, reading aloud combined with tape recording, and reading silently. Each child was screened neurologically, and the electrical potentials recorded from the scalp for normal EEG investigations and, in addition, for a proprioceptive task, while reading silently and aloud, and for special visual stimuli, which could be used to stimulate the whole of each quadrant of the visual field. All the children were assessed by the teaching staff, the relevant background situations were considered, and as much as possible done in the way of formal educational and psychological tests.

In this group of thirty-three children studied, eight were receiving remedial reading training and another three were very much poorer than average performers. The total number of second year juniors was thirty- seven, but four had to be eliminated because of absence for various reasons during this survey.

General

A good clinician needs to learn to be aware of his patient as a whole—not just his immediate professional speciality—as does the child's teachers. One cannot, therefore, always easily isolate one particular facet of function and behaviour, without bearing in mind that there may be other anomalous aspects which are likely to have a bearing on that function.

Case history A (no. 10)

This boy was left-handed, with some ambidexterity, but was quite a good performer. His IQ was 105, his RQ 112, spelling 10 out of 10, and motivation good. He tended to hesitate and miss a line on reading aloud; his writing was untidy; and there was an earlier history of reversals on writing. He tended to close his right eye sometimes during near vision, and had a general stressed appearance. He exhibited no sense of order on the Macdonald Critchley test. On investigation he was found to be left-eye dominant, but tended to switch quickly from one eye to the other, with the fixing eye diverging and then overconverging, and the other eye divergent.

He had normal visual acuity, with negligible refractive error. His eye-movement recording was unsteadier on reading aloud, with increased vertical movement of the eyes, and much saccadic movement of the left eye.

Through effort and practice and by enjoying reading to himself, he was able to contain his basic convergence weakness, and achieve quite a good performance in view of his ocular handicaps. By sometimes closing his right eye, he was able to avoid the right-eye image confusing that of the left eye, when he could not achieve adequate binocular coordination.

His mistakes and hesitancy in reading could tend to coincide, for example, with when he was switching from one eye to the other. By switching quickly, he was able to achieve quite a reasonable reading performance.

Eye-movement recordings of case A reading aloud and silently

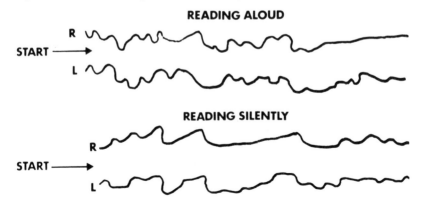

READING ALOUD

START → R

L

READING SILENTLY

R

START →

L

Case history B (no. 25)

This girl was a very poor reader who paused frequently, hesitated and made mistakes. There was a fair amount of head movement, with a tendency to turn the head to the left.

She was in the remedial reading class and was linguistically deprived, as her family were Italians. She had an IQ of 107, RQ of 81, and her spelling score was 2 out of 10. She had poor motivation, was regarded as very lazy, and had a poor upbringing.

She exhibited mixed-eye dominance, but normal left to right order. Vision was normal in the right eye, and slightly less in the left due to some astigmatism. She had considerable difficulty in maintaining convergence, tending to switch from one eye to the other with alteration of head posture.

Here was a child, therefore, with some ocular similarity to Case A reported earlier but who, through lack of motivation and effort, combined with a poor background, remained a very poor achiever.

Ocular significance of posture

In any class, children will have very many different attitudes of posture. Sometimes a fixed trend will be evident; in another case the child may appear almost to be searching for a suitable position, for example, a child may have his head on one side, or even rest the side of his head on his desk. Though it may be sensible to correct these postural anomalies, it may be helpful to consider why they may arise.

In my experience the younger the child the more difficulty he has in trying to coordinate the eyes for the convergence effort required for near vision, i.e. he is binocularly unstable. Also the dominance situation as a whole, and between the eyes, appears to be less established. If, therefore, these two situations exist, the child may well exhibit some manifestation of binocular image confusion. The images may then at times be falling on retinal areas that do not correspond, i.e. are not linked together neurologically to perceive a single combined image. At the worst under these circumstances the child may even momentarily see double.

Case history C (no. 2)

Writing posture of Case C

This girl had an RQ of 106, considerably lower than would be expected from an IQ of 124. Her teacher regarded her as average and a pleasant but somewhat placid child, with good motivation. She still finger-pointed while reading, exhibiting some head movement, and had a small palpebral aperture, indicating stress.

She had normal vision right and left, and passed the stereoscopic test on the vision screener. During reading she tended to diverge and overconverge with one eye, with the other eye diverging. She also tended to switch eyes. A situation of uncertain dominance at near vision, and difficulty of maintaining binocular coordination of the eyes on convergence together could help to account for a poorer reading achievement. Her posture would indicate that she would have difficulty with image confusion.

In other cases, the child may be turning his head in such a way that he can more readily maintain some stability of alignment of the eyes. There could be a tendency to try and maintain steady central fixation of a dominant eye and allow the other eye to drift out. The image will then fall on a more eccentric area of the latter eye, where the visual acuity is lower, and fusional area larger. In consequence less binocular confusion will be produced.

Case history D (no. 1)
Case D reading

This girl was a good performer, and well motivated. She tended to close her right eye during near vision, read fast aloud, and adopted a posture of leaning over to the right.

She had normal vision right and left, and passed the stereoscopic test on the vision screener. Dominance at distance was undecided, and for near vision tended to be left-eye dominant. She exhibited a reversed sense of order.

During reading she attempted to use her left eye more than her right, and had difficulty in maintaining convergence. She showed greater unsteadiness of eye-movement in both eyes when reading aloud than when reading silently. She adopted a posture which allowed her to use her left eye as stably as possible, and which may at times have allowed the nose to cut off vision from the right eye.

Case history E (no. 14)
Case E reading

This boy was a poor reader, with below average intelligence and reading quotient, and just average spelling. Motivation was below average. Reading aloud showed effort combined with slowness and mistakes. When reading he exhibited jerky head movements, combined with marked rotation of the head to the right, and had a small palpebral aperture.

He had normal vision in both eyes, and passed the stereoscopic test on the vision screener. He was right-eye dominant, but because of a tendency for the eyes to diverge at near vision, his head posture to the right helped him to maintain a somewhat steadier fixation with the right eye, and allowed the left eye to diverge. He tended to switch eyes while making small jerky head movements. Because of his difficulty in maintaining alignment of the eyes for near vision, a good reading performance would be difficult from the visual point of view.

Laterality and eye dominance
In general, the younger the child, the less decided appears to be eye dominance. When this uncertainty persists, and the child seems to be ambidextrous and ambi-eyed, there may be some association of undecided dominance with poor reading ability, particularly if there is difficulty in maintaining binocular alignment of the eyes. Investigation of eye dominance is more difficult than may generally be assumed. Many tests involve a proprioceptive element that may influence results, as also may the distance and position at which objects are viewed. In this investigation, therefore, in addition to two classical tests for eye dominance both for distance and for near, how the eyes viewed in the different directions of gaze was also noted, particularly at the postural position most likely to be adopted.

The light-threshold contrasts for each eye were also assessed for the fovea, macular, and central areas up to 25° eccentricity. The evoked electrical potentials produced from the brain for different types of visual stimuli are also being studied to obtain better information about the cerebral aspects of eye dominance. There have been many studies regarding laterality and educational performance (Clark 1957 and Vernon 1957) but I feel that the subject is very complex and must also, for example, include binocular and cerebral aspects.

Of the thirty-three eight year old children examined in this present study, eighteen showed unsettled dominance. Out of a total of eleven, eight were very poor readers, and an additional three had a below average reading achievement. Of the remaining seven, four had an achievement of just above average, and the remaining three were quite good.

Case history F (no. 31)

This West Indian girl was in a remedial class and was linguistically deprived. She had an IQ of 86, an RQ of less than 79, and a spelling attainment of 1 out of 10. Her motivation was good, but she was a very poor reader, making long pauses and mistakes. She exhibited very considerable head movements, with head tilt to the right during reading.

She was right-handed, but exhibited an ambi-eyed situation, with a mixed sense of order. She had normal vision, assessed on a letter chart, but a vision screener could not be used because of poor comprehension.

During reading, both eyes tended to diverge because of difficulty in maintaining convergence. There was a variable and unequal eye movement, combined with a tendency to switch eyes in association with a head tilt and twist to one side, and then the other. Here, therefore, a situation of undecided dominance, unstable binocular coordination and poor convergence ability, in association with a difficult background situation with language deprivation, are handicapping the child, even though she did make quite a considerable effort.

Eye-movement recording of Case F

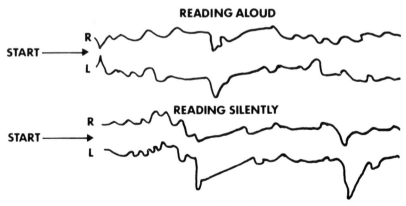

Whether a child is right-handed or left-handed, or tries to use the left or the right eye most, can have a considerable bearing on posture for near vision. Naturally if a child is to write left-handed, it is important that the eye is sufficiently far over to the right so that the child can see what he is writing without vision being occluded by the pencil. If the child tries to use the left eye in preference to the right eye, a more extreme posture to the right will be necessary to enable the left eye to be used readily. In addition there may be rotation and/or twist of the head to enable a more stable binocular situation.

Case history G (no. 30)
Case G writing

This boy was left-handed, and tended to come close to his task, with his head tilted and turned to the right. If he tried he could achieve better than average attainment, but was impulsive, and spoilt at home. He tended to read fast, with some jerkiness and mistakes.

He tended to be left-eye dominant, and had difficulty in maintaining convergence. He was inclined to blink excessively. Holding his head close to his work, and employing an extreme position to the right helped him to concentrate with his left dominant eye. Vision from the right eye was thus almost occluded by his nose, thereby reducing a tendency for image confusion when he could not maintain his eyes in alignment. Also his head twist would help him to maintain more steady fixation with his left eye.

Sense of order
Reading and writing in European languages is from left to right. If children do not have a settled left to right sense of order, it appears reasonable to assume that they could have more difficulty in reading, spelling and writing.

A useful test is that devised by Macdonald Critchley. In the centre of a card there is a cross, and on each side of the cross are four coloured discs. The child has to look at the cross and then name the colours in the order in which he sees them. Four out of thirty-three children exhibited no sense of order, and three of these four were below average performers in reading.

Movement of the head

Some children may exhibit a considerable degree of head movement while reading. If this is combined with difficulty in maintaining coordination of the eyes, movement of the head can be associated with a tendency to switch to use one eye more than the other, and possibly back again. This appears especially likely if there is an uncertain dominance relationship between the eyes. Unless the child can achieve this switching of the eyes quite quickly, a tendency to hesitate and make mistakes while reading aloud may be evident with these head movements.

Of the thirty-three children examined, nine exhibited excessive head movement during reading. Of these, eight were poor readers. With this group exhibiting excessive head movement, there was a tendency to switch eyes as the head moved from one side to the other. In addition, seven out of these eight children exhibited unsettled eye dominance.

Case history H (no. 29)

This girl was in a remedial group, and was of West Indian origin. Her reading attainment was below that which would have been expected from her intelligence. She made considerable effort to read, and was quite good under the circumstances, exhibiting as she did some hesitancy, jerkiness, pauses, and regressions. During reading she demonstrated excessive head movement with a marked turn to the left.

She had normal vision in both eyes, but tended to vary between left-eye dominance to an ambi-eye situation. In addition to unsettled eye dominance, she had considerable difficulty in trying to maintain convergence for near vision. She tended to switch eyes in association with excessive head movements. Her ocular situation would therefore undoubtedly help to produce a poorer reading attainment than would have been expected of her from her intelligence.

Signs of ocular stress

If children are observed when reading or working at their desks, signs of ocular stress can sometimes be noticed. Common instances are general appearance of tension, including frowning, screwing up the eyes, and excessive blinking. In some cases these signs may be due to the need for a refractive correction, or a difficulty in using both eyes together, usually in maintaining convergence.

As these stress signs are indication of excessive effort, the child's performance could be quite good in spite of an ocular weakness. However, even then one would expect difficulty in maintaining performance when the child tires, when, for example, reading can become hesitant and writing untidy.

Of the six children exhibiting stress signs, two had a below average reading attainment, and four out of these six hesitated and made mistakes on reading aloud.

Case history I (no. 15)

This boy tended to screw his eyes up and blink during near vision. Reading aloud tended to be jerky and with mistakes. His reading attainment was below what would have been expected for his intelligence, and he had good motivation.

His vision in both eyes was normal, and he had negligible refractive error. His eye dominance was uncertain both at close range and at distance. During reading he tended to switch eyes, exhibiting a divergence/convergence situation in an effort to maintain his convergence. His lower achievement for reading than would have been expected, and also a tendency for discomfort during near vision, could be considerably influenced by effort in controlling poor convergence and difficulty from unsettled dominance.

Conclusions

These illustrations of just a part of the work in which I have been concerned, suggest that ocular and postural anomalies do bear a considerable relationship to how the child might perform in class, and to some of the difficulties that he may exhibit. Some of the situations discussed in this paper do take a considerable degree of experience, and often sophisticated equipment, to investigate adequately. However, in the more obvious cases, after a suitable investigation binocular visual training exercises may be enough to help the child, for example the use of polarized vectograms, (Stereo Optical, Chicago) whereby the right and left eyes can each only see one of the slides at a time. The slides can be overlapped and moved independently.

It is hoped that this paper will help teachers to recognize visual and ocular situations which may be affecting the child's progress and, in general, encourage a greater interest in this field of clinical work.

Acknowledgments

I would like to acknowledge the helpful cooperation of D. C. Binney and colleagues, and Mr G. Raisin, and his staff, in this project. Thanks are due also to Miss G. Powell-Cullingford, and Miss P. Smith, for part of their clinical work with me while students at the University, and to the technical staff of the Department for their help in construction of some of the equipment needed. I would also like to acknowledge the help given by The Worshipful Company of Spectacle Makers towards this clinical project.

References

CLARK, M. M. (1957) *Left-Handedness: Laterality Characteristics and their Educational Implications* Scottish Council for Research in Education No 39 London: University of London Press

CRITCHLEY, M. (1964) *Developmental Dyslexia* London: Heinemann

VERNON, M. D. (1957) *Backwardness in Reading: A Study of its Nature and Origin* London: Cambridge University Press

10 The analysis and assessment of reading comprehension

Fergus McBride

The nature of comprehension

Traditionally learning to read has been thought of as involving the mastery of two more or less easily distinguished categories of processes—learning the 'mechanics' of reading and understanding or getting meaning. It is significant, I believe, that it was customary to talk of 'learning the mechanics of reading' but not of 'learning to understand', the assumption being that mechanics could be taught and therefore were learnable, while understanding just happened as the result of 'mastering the mechanics'. For example Sir Cyril Burt (1923) wrote of his word recognition test which appeared in *Mental and Scholastic Tests,* 'the foregoing tests of reading measure either mere mechanical accuracy or else mere fluency and speed . . . those that follow measure comprehension, that is, the ability to read with understanding'. What the term 'the mechanics of reading' includes is determined largely by the convictions of the teacher regarding the nature of those processes which must necessarily intervene between the sight of print and understanding. It is, therefore, a nebulous term which may include decoding at the grapheme-phoneme level, word recognition, predictive and structuring operations or whatever the links in the chain linking sense with sound and sight are considered to be.

The importance of comprehension is generally recognized though methods of teaching have often neglected its development; but the nature of the process of comprehending is little understood. Comprehension may occur as the result of experiences involving either spoken or written language and in the latter case it is called 'reading comprehension'. It is not known, and may never be known, what the nature of the processes by which the brain makes meaning from the grapho-phonic and syntactic clues available on the printed page are, nor has anyone formulated a satisfactory definition of 'meaning'; one cannot yet describe accurately what it is one is trying to measure in reading tests of 'understanding'. Yet, teachers must come to some conclusions as to what comprehension involves in order to help the children to develop this essential competence.

Many years ago Huey (1908) illustrated that meaning was not necessarily associated with imagery and wrote, 'The consciousness of meaning itself belongs in the main to that group of mental states, the feelings, which I regard with Wundt as unanalyzable, or at least having a large unanalyzable core or body.' Modern psycholinguists are equally prepared to leave unattempted a precise definition of comprehension. Frank Smith (1971) writes, 'The attempt to find a single definition of all the various and idiosyncratic aspects of meaning is a rack on which many theoretical vessels have foundered.' But Huey and James anticipated the modern ideas of 'surface' and 'deep' levels of language—the physical manifestations in print or sound and the underlying semantic structure or meaning. The correspondence between the two levels is not simple and is not understood. Just as we structure visually an ambiguous picture in different ways so we may structure verbally an ambiguous sentence in different ways, for example, 'The chicken was too hot to eat.' Again the same meaning may be conveyed by different surface manifestations, for example, 'The boys hit the dog' and 'The dog was hit by the boys.'

The teacher's basic problem is to promote a linking of surface features with comprehending and that of the test constructor is to assess the extent to which this is taking place. Most children have acquired a fairly high level of competence in oral language before beginning to learn to read. Most children have learned to link sense and oral surface features spontaneously and independently and it may be assumed that apart from the difference in medium, comprehending written and spoken language is a similar process. The development of competence in oral language involving familiarity with the patterns and syntax of the language and with an extensive array of concepts is, therefore, a necessary foundation for progress in reading competence. In teaching reading it is assumed that if the children are taught the recognition of surface features, they will spontaneously develop the ability to achieve meaning. Since comprehending is mental behaviour and not overtly manifested, the teacher can only infer the degree to which comprehension is taking or has taken place by noting the child's responses to other verbal data—for example, to a question or an instruction from the teacher or book.

Comprehending for different purposes

The nature of the comprehension processes involved is also modified by the purposes of the reader. The fact that printed language is available to the reader at his discretion (as contrasted with speech which is transient) permits a wide variety of reading techniques differing in speed and intensity—strategies which cannot be applied in comprehending spoken language. The adult reads a novel because he believes it to be an interesting story, a biographical or historical novel because he has an interest in the person or the period or in order that he may increase his knowledge or find enjoyment in the process. Perhaps he has formulated this purpose on the basis of a recommendation of a friend or from what he has read on the cover of the book. The adult reads a book on floral art or the manual on car maintenance because he wishes to equip himself to do something or to improve his skill in some practical activity. The adult reads the newspaper article because he has an interest in the political, economic or educational issues being currently discussed in our society, with a view to formulating an opinion of his own on the topic. The student in school, university or workshop reads information to achieve relatively permanent knowledge of the topic he is studying. Insofar as the reading of adults satisfies their needs and achieves their purposes their reading is satisfactory. When one compares adult reading, where purposes are consciously or unconsciously set by the reader, with many practices prevalent in schools we find many contrasts. School reading books are often read just because they are there. Some have exercises or questions which follow the reading material, with the result that the children have to 'reread' the material before being able to answer the questions. Even in reading tests we find unsatisfactory instructions such as, 'Read the following and answer the questions below'. Often the child's approach to this task is to read the questions first—and with good reason. The validity of such reading comprehension tests is very questionable; they fail to recognize that we read differently for different purposes. Thorndike (1917) initiated a long period of thinking by educationists about the nature of reading comprehension in an article which he called 'Reading as reasoning'. He focusses attention on the fact that little thought had been given to the dynamics of comprehension and that the notion of understanding being gradually built up from the meaning of the elements, just as one builds a wall from bricks, was an inadequate explanation of the process of comprehension. He illustrates empirically that reading is a very elaborate process, which involves weighing each of the many elements in the sentence, their organization in the proper relationship to one another, the selection of certain of their connotations and the rejection of others which leads to the comprehension of the whole. But he emphasizes in particular that all this takes place 'under the influence of the right *mental set* or *purposes* or demand'. He then went on to advocate the substitution of silent reading practice followed by questions or summarizing exercises for the oral reading practice which was predominant in classrooms then, 'the vice of the poor reader is to say the words to himself actively making judgments concerning their meaning. Reading aloud or listening to one reading aloud may leave this vice unaltered or even encouraged.'

There is substantial evidence from research that the skilled reader uses different strategies according to his purposes at the time. For example Helen Smith (1967) compared the strategies used by good and poor readers in reading for different purposes. 'Good' readers were those who scored above the seventieth percentile and 'poor' readers were below the thirtieth percentile, on the test used. She found that the good readers employed different procedures when they read for widely divergent purposes—in this case for details and for general impressions. Poor readers tended not to differentiate their approach in the two types of reading task. Sixty years ago, William S. Gray photographed the eye movements of adult readers when they were reading prose for the purpose of reproducing the content and again when they were reading for the purposes of answering subsequent questions. He concluded that the processes involved in the two tasks were different and that the more expert the reader the more flexible he was in using different skills. Clearly the conclusion from these investigations is that in teaching reading, the purpose for reading should always be kept in mind. This does not mean that the teacher should always provide the purpose, for children will often have their own purposes, but she should ascertain through discussion whether the pupil's reading is purposeful, what the purposes were and whether these purposes were achieved. In testing reading the purposes for reading should be stated before giving the 'blanket' instruction 'Read the following passage'.

Types of comprehending

If, as has been stated, skilled readers employ different reading strategies according to their purposes, then logically the next question is 'What are the different strategies or reading skills which together make up comprehension?' Are there as many subskills as the 215 purposes which Helen Smith (1967) referred to? Or are they reducible to a more manageable minimum which can be described, named, and hence taught and even measured? Attempts between 1944 and the present to answer these questions have been of two main types: empirical and *a priori*. Empirical approaches are those which examine children's performances (in quantifiable terms) on different types of reading tasks and by means of factorial analysis of the correlations between the scores on the different reading tasks an attempt is made to determine common factors which will 'explain' the correlations. Of course, the different types of reading incorporated in the tests themselves are determined *a priori;* for example Roger T. Lennon (1962) summarized researches to that time of the factorial type. Davies, who carried out an experiment which is a classical example of this approach, included nine reading skills in his tests. The factorial analysis of the results yielded five significant factors. Thurstone questioned these findings and maintained that one factor was all that was required to explain the intercorrelations; hence, in his view, reading comprehension was largely composed of one element. Similar factorial studies have been carried out by Langson using six reading tests yielding fourteen scores, and Conant tried to answer the question, 'Is there a general reading comprehension or does reading proficiency depend upon a variety of independent skills?' Intercorrelations in Conant's investigation were above .5 with the exception of five intercorrelations which led her to conclude, 'Students in general use relatively *independent* abilities in this study-type reading.' Artley found the intercorrelations between the specific measures to lie between .6 and .8 and concluded that one could not dismiss the possibility that there are a great number of pupils who might profit from a specific type of instruction and that there exists a significant degree of specificity in the measures relating to reading comprehension. Harris, after carrying out a similar experiment, concluded that one and only one ability is common to the comprehension of literary passages of different types and one general factor is adequate to account for all the intercorrelations. Stoker and Kropp found intercorrelations between tests designed to measure different reading abilities of .67 to .76 and ruled out the concepts of differentiable reading abilities, at least as measured by the Iowa Tests of Educational Development.

Kerfoot (1967) after reviewing many similar studies, said of the results of such analyses, 'They are at once confounding and useful . . . they present a problem of inconsistency in both theoretical base and descriptive terminology', and Farr (1969) confesses that there has been a failure to delineate the basic measurable components of reading comprehension satisfacorily.

The comprehension skills which are analysed are limited to those which are included in the tests administered, and what is testable in reading covers a much narrower area than what is teachable and learnable. Therefore, until it is possible to measure a much wider gamut of reading abilities than is at present possible, factorial studies must remain of limited use. There is an obvious parallel here with the factorial studies relating to the measurement of 'intelligence' and the conflict between those who found one all-prevading factor and those who maintained that intelligence comprised distinct and different specific factors. 'Intelligence' became a meaningless term for many and we ended by defining intelligence as 'whatever is measured by intelligence tests'. A suggestion along the same lines with regard to comprehension has been made by Kerfoot (1968) who recommended that, in order to avoid confusion in terminology, teachers and testers should concentrate upon reading operations which can be exemplified and ignore generalized titles for tests of hypothetical reading skills. Finally, it is highly speculative to conclude that because there are positive intercorrelations between performances on tests calling for different abilities there are operational entities corresponding to these factors.

A priori attempts to identify different types of reading fall into at least three types: classification by the unit of the reading material, for example word, sentence and paragraph comprehension; by the amount of care devoted upon the reading and by the nature of the process assumed to operate, e.g. reading for literal meaning, inferential or interpretive reading, critical reading and creative reading.

It is impossible to interpret this complex array of studies in any one operational way for teachers in order that they may design teaching procedures to promote comprehension, or for test makers in order that they may design tests to measure the components of reading ability. Yet these analyses reveal the complexity of the concept of comprehension, and one must disentangle certain elements in comprehension which we believe to be important and worthy of promotion by conscious efforts. As Farr (1969) says, 'The classroom teacher needs some kind of operational definition or at least some idea of what is involved in reading in order to proceed with instruction.'

Reading is a language skill and in reading we are substituting a visual medium for the auditory one; reading is a process in which the reader recognizes language which he has already acquired. If he has not acquired the language he cannot recognize it. If the concepts and language used by the writer have not been acquired by the reader, he will not be in a position to understand the message. The development of competence in oral language is an essential prerequisite for efficient reading. That is, vocabulary development and familiarity with the patterns of sentence and the combination of words need to be developed in oral language as useful *per se and* as a foundation for reading.

The nature of assessment

The accepted principles of assessment in reading are being seriously questioned at the present time. Traditionally, attainment tests in reading had to conform to the established criteria of validity, reliability, standardization and norms. Millman (1972) emphasizes the dichotomy between conventional 'norm-referenced' tests and 'criterion-referenced' tests, 'Unlike norm-referenced tests in which scores get meaning from norms indicating how well other students have performed on a test, criterion-referenced measurement meaning comes from a comparison of the students' performance relative to the skills being assessed by the test questions.' Carver (1972) makes a similar distinction between conventional psychometric testing with its emphasis upon differences between individuals and 'edumetric' testing which would emphasize progressive within-individual gains.

This new thinking about the testing of reading should be welcomed insofar as it emphasizes the important part played by the teachers in their day to day informal assessment and diagnoses of the child's reading, and at the same time highlights the need for improving the validity of tests made on conventional lines and hence indicating the type of teaching required by the child. One would hope, nevertheless, that criterion-referenced tests would be valid, discriminating and reliable instruments. However, it is clear that not every test requires to be calibrated on a representative sample of the whole nation.

It is one thing to decide that a certain skill is an important element in reading ability and quite another to devise a means of testing whether a child has this skill or not. Often the operations called for in testing bear little resemblance to operations in reading in a context beyond that of testing. When this happens there are grounds for questioning the validity of the test. Furthermore this kind of test gives little help as to the type of teaching required by the pupil.

When a device has been designed to measure a type of reading skill, the question of the pupils developing a specific facility in carrying out this type of exercise arises. Vernon (1962) found that assessments of the understanding of complex concepts were affected by factors arising from the method of testing and recommended that inclusion in a test of reading ability should be that the operations used in the testing situation should resemble as far as possible the operations involved in the reading situation.

The Edinburgh Reading Tests

The foregoing were some of the considerations borne in mind in the construction of The Edinburgh Reading Test, Stage 3 (McBride 1973).

In the first place it was thought necessary to provide the classroom teacher with a professional instrument which would enable her to determine her children's competence level in reading. Second, it was agreed that the test should be diagnostic in the sense that the result of testing would indicate where teaching was called for and what type of teaching was required.

The fundamental rationale of the approach adopted in the test was that by age 10:0 to 12:6 children read for a variety of purposes and their reading strategies vary with their purposes.

So in Stage 3 of The Edinburgh Reading Tests there are five ten-minute subtests as follows:

1   Reading for items of information.
2   Understanding a series of sentences and the semantic relationships between them.
3   Selecting and retaining the main ideas in descriptive and expository material.
4   Comprehending points of view on various matters of opinion.
5   Matching context with the meaning of words and phrases.

The scores of the pupils on all subtests together are converted to a Standardized Reading Score which indicates the pupil's overall competence in reading compared with children of the same age in England, Wales or in Scotland. In order that the teacher may match the children's ability with reading materials of suitable difficulty, these overall scores may be converted to Reading Ages which are limited to the age range of the children in the standardized sample.

The pupil's scores on the five individual subtests are represented on a profile sheet by standardized scores and a simple procedure has been devised which will indicate the strengths and weaknesses of individual pupils and of the whole class in the types of reading incorporated in the test.

In interpreting the scores of pupils on this test the teacher should keep in mind that the tests cover only a small area of reading abilities and whilst the results are very probably indicative of other areas of reading not sampled by the test, the subtests do not provide a blueprint of the skills, habits and attitudes the teacher is working to promote. The tests employ testing devices rather than teaching devices and whilst an attempt has been made to use items which involve operations similar to those employed in reading, it is doubtful whether practice in some of the exercises involved in the test will promote the types of reading competence which the test was intended to measure.

Scores on the Edinburgh Reading Test
The level of the overall reading ability of the class as indicated by the standardized reading scores provides the teacher with an index of the achievement of the class generally in relation to children of the same age throughout the country and will indicate the degree to which the children's progress in reading merits special attention and additional time.

Whilst the analysis of class performances on the subtests will show any weaknesses or strengths in specific subtests which exist in the class as a whole, the standardized reading scores and reading ages of the individual pupils will help teachers to match the pupil's reading ability with the difficulty level of the reading materials, and the profiles of individual children will indicate the extent to which the child's Reading Quotient is the result of a consistent performance on all subtests or whether there are marked divergencies in some subtest scores.

Teaching indicated by the test
Where a low standardized reading score is the result of consistently low performances on all the subtests it will be necessary to ascertain the extent to which the pupil has made progress in the basic skills of reading and to provide help where necessary.

A poor overall performance may be the result of an impoverished or defective development of general competence in language or of a combination of this and poor reading skill, in which case the priority would be to provide experiences and teaching to enrich the pupil's mastery of language.

All pupils will require a programme of reading activities which caters for the development of a wide variety of reading competencies and also involves the pupil in reading in connection with the study of the other topics. Pupils showing specific weaknesses in certain subtests will require special teaching in the area of their weakness as well as in the furtherance of their reading skills generally. The question arises should the teacher provide specific practice in selected reading skill in order to improve the child's competence in that skill? Helen Smith (1966) found that specific practice in separate reading skills did improve the pupil's performance in those skills. The danger is, however, that an overemphasis of exercises to develop specific skills may become a dull, monotonous and apparently purposeless drill. We should not, however, regard a specific exercise designed to promote a type of reading and the use of such a reading procedure in the context of the pursuit of a wider goal as mutually exclusive alternatives. Success and satisfaction in specific exercises will offset unfavourable reaction to drill and mastery of strategies and techniques acquired by conscious practice are appreciated when they are demanded by a situation involving reading.

References
BURT, C. (1923) *Handbook of Tests* preface and pp. XI and XIII
CARVER, R. P. (1972) Reading tests in 1970 versus 1980: Psychometric versus edumetric *The Reading Teacher* 26, 3
FARR, R. (1969) *Reading: what can be measured?* Newark, Delaware: IRA
HUEY, E. B. (1908) *The Psychology and Pedagogy of Reading* New York: Macmillan (reprinted 1965 MIT Press)
KERFOOT, J. F. (1968) 'Problems and research considerations in reading comprehension' in M. A. Dawson *Developing Comprehension* Newark, Delaware: IRA

LENNON, R. T. (1962) *The Reading Teacher* 15, 6

MILLMAN, J. (1972) Criterion-referenced measurement, an alternative *The Reading Teacher* 26, 3

McBRIDE, F. and McNAUGHT, P. (1973) *Teachers Manual for Stage 3 Edinburgh Reading Tests* London: University of London Press

SMITH, F. (1971) *Understanding Reading* New York: Holt, Rinehart and Winston

SMITH, H. K. (1966) *Cooperative Research Project No. 1714* Chicago: University of Chicago Press

SMITH, H. (1967) The responses of good and poor readers when asked to read for different purposes *Reading Research Quarterly* 3, 1

THORNDIKE, E. L. (1917) Reading as reasoning: a study of mistakes in paragraph reading *The Journal of Educational Psychology* 8, 6 reprinted in J. Merritt and A. Melnik (Eds) *Reading, Today and Tomorrow* Milton Keynes: Open University Press

11 Approaching reading in the middle school

Donald Moyle

Introduction

Education would appear to have two major tasks, namely to satisfy the needs of the pupil in terms of both the present and the future. It would seem that there has been a tendency at various times to lean very heavily towards the one or the other. There is little reason, however, for the two sets of needs to be mutually exclusive; both can be combined and indeed must be if the educative process is to be effective.

The teaching of reading has certainly suffered from the tendency to favour one set of needs. When this happens the child is given a set of skills he sees little use for and has little motivation to employ or he lacks the skills necessary to expand his learning through reading.

The reading curriculum

The reading curriculum has three major elements: skills and strategies, purposes and media. If reading is to play a helpful part in education as a whole it is essential that all three are given attention at all stages of development. This is not to say that at any one period every aspect of reading must be included. From time to time the weighting towards each one will vary.

Reading skills and strategies

The following represents a summary list of skills and strategies that must be mastered if the pupil is to become an effective reader in any situation which he may meet in adult life. All these should be developing during the nine to thirteen years period of schooling. As this can only be a summary, the reader's attention is drawn to more extensive lists which can be found in Russell (1961), Clymer (1972) and Strang (1972). Russell and Strang give age ranges at which each group of skills should be given special attention.

Word attack skills

1 The use of linguistic knowledge to discover the function of the unknown word in the sentence.
2 The use of context to find the meaning of the unknown word.
3 The use of a knowledge of the spelling rules and sound/symbol relationships.
4 The use of memory facility relating the unknown word to words memorized by their pattern of some significant feature.

As none of the four groups of skills outlined above are fool-proof when used alone, the effective reader must be able to combine all the skills to obtain the result most likely to be accurate.

Comprehension skills
1 Literal comprehension. The ability to answer the question 'What did the author say?'
2 Interpretive comprehension. The translation of the language of the author and the rearrangement of his ideas so that the reader can answer the question 'What did the author mean?'
3 Evaluative and appreciative comprehension. The detailed examination of the material at intellectual and emotional thinking levels in relation to the reader's previous knowledge and present needs.
4 Integration and memorization. The selection and memorization of those facts and ideas the reader wishes to retain and add to previously gained understanding.
5 Action. Making use of the results of the reading and thinking undertaken.

Necessarily, there is an overlap between effective usage of comprehension skills and the purposes for which they were applied and the type of reading media used.

Search skills
The reader must be able to find those materials most likely to enable him to achieve his purposes:

1 library skills
2 survey skills to judge relevance of individual books etc
3 reference skills.

Reading strategies
Having found the appropriate materials the reader must make decisions about how the reading will be undertaken in the light of his purpose. There are three major groups of strategies:

1 intensive reading for study purposes
2 scanning for specific items of information
3 skimming for general impression.

Reading purposes
Merritt (1971) has suggested that the following five headings can subsume the purposes which can arise in reality situations:

1 home and family
2 employment
3 leisure

4 consumer
5 community.

Each one includes many subheadings and there can be considerable over-lap between them. Experience has shown, however, that this simple list can be of considerable value in planning work, is equally applicable to tasks in adult life and the middle school, and is also a useful check on whether the full range of purposes are regularly being employed within the class-room. They can also form the basis of a storage or filing system for materials.

The reader must be able to plan his reading in relation to his purposes. This involves the ability to delineate the various aspects of his purpose and set the questions which he needs to answer. A method of approaching this is set out in detail by Farnes (1973).

Reading media
Schools are often somewhat overconcerned with the use of books. The adult reader must be able to process a variety of media. These may be associated with different types of purpose and need special skills or strate-gies for efficient usage. We do children less than justice therefore in terms of skill-development and reading experience if the range of media used in school is too narrow. To be aware of the range of media available helps the teacher and pupil to plan work more scientifically, aids in the estimation of the usefulness of a particular source and in delineating the skills which are appropriate to its usage.

The following classifications have proved helpful in teaching children about the range of media and the approach to them that is likely to be most fruitful.

Classification by author purpose

To inform	e.g. academic text
To entertain	e.g. novel
To persuade	e.g. religious tract
To elicit information	e.g. questionnaire
To proscribe	e.g. legal document
To prescribe	e.g. instruction booklet

(Merritt and Moyle 1972)

Classification by type of writing

Descriptive	static	e.g. house specification
	dynamic	e.g. car production
Rhetorical	inductive	e.g. research paper
	deductive	e.g. literary criticism
Imperative		e.g. insurance policy
Interrogative		e.g. test
Exclamatory		e.g. political pamphlet

(Farnes and Melnik 1972)

Media types
Fiction books
Notices
Advertisements
Letters
Brochures
Newspapers
Journals
Magazines
Regulations
Forms and questionnaires
Pamphlets
Legal documents
Reports and minutes

Issues in the planning of the reading curriculum

The reading curriculum is composed of a complex array of skills and strategies on the one hand and the content or areas where the skills can be applied on the other. Parker (1964) has called these two aspects skill-getting and skill-using. He suggests that when the child works in situations entirely devised by the teacher skill-getting can be well catered for. The teacher can set a sequence for the learning of the various skills. However, it could be that though the skills are learned the child will not, in such a situation, have sufficient opportunities to find out when and how to apply them. In a more informal, child-centred situation where the child selects learning tasks the opportunity for realistic application of reading skills is present. Parker suggests, however, that all too often this approach leads to children becoming involved in tasks which they cannot complete satisfactorily because they have not mastered the skills essential to its completion.

There are two interlinked problems here: sequence in which skills are most helpfully learned and whether a skill learned in one situation will be transferred to other similar situations at a later date. Parker suggests that all skills develop in a linear manner but if there is a perfect or even best order for the development of the subskills in reading it has yet to be discovered. There appears therefore to be the opportunity for great variation in the order in which skills can be mastered and these seem to relate to the individuality of the pupil and the tasks in which he is engaged.

The ability to select the appropriate skills and strategies to employ in an hitherto unfamiliar learning situation would seem to depend largely upon the width of opportunity given previously to plan reading tasks. Similar purposes have similar skills associated with them and therefore the association of skills with reading purposes is an important facility which must be encouraged within school.

Two possible approaches

We must make provision for the development of skills and the ability to know where and when to apply them. There would seem to be two major lines of attack.

Starting with the skills
Here a sequence of skills is presented by the teacher or through a set of materials such as a reading laboratory. The teacher can be certain what skills are mastered and diagnose easily individual difficulties. On the other hand the skills may not be applied elsewhere, they may not always be matched to the learning preferences of the individual and motivation may be low due to a feeling that the work is merely being undertaken for its own sake or to please the teacher.

Such difficulties can be overcome to some extent by ensuring that the skills taught are immediately employed by the child in a wider situation. For example, a child showing interest in the content of a power builder within an SRA *Reading Laboratory* can build on his skills through pursuing a topic in the same area (for an example of how this can be arranged see Moyle 1970).

Starting with the content
If the child starts from a reading purpose then motivation should be high and the possibility of transfer of skill-learning greater. There are dangers however. The teacher must know the children very well and be able to see exactly what the needs of any situation are and relate the stage of development reached by the individual child to them. One can see that in a busy classroom the teacher is going to be very hard worked.

Working in this way does not mean that the child has to master all skills in a skill-using situation. There will still be a place for teaching and for structured materials, but both will be employed within an activity where they will be used and the child can see the need to master them.

It will be important that both teacher and child work out in detail the questions related to the main purpose, the resources to be used and the skills associated with them. A table such as that on page 96 seems convenient for this purpose.

Children can develop a planning strategy of their own using a curriculum development approach suggested by Merritt (1971):

Goals	What do I want to do?
Plans	How can I best achieve my goals?
Implementation	How must I proceed?
	Did I achieve my goals?
Development	What should I do next?

At the planning stage there will be two sections, one dealing with the content, the other how the content should be used. It is at this point that teacher and child need to reflect whether the child already has the necessary skills, whether he will be able to master them whilst achieving his purpose or whether some preparatory skill-learning work is needed. In the latter case a devised learning situation e.g. the use of programmed instruction, is acceptable for it is undertaken as part of the achievement of the original purpose and will be practised within a skill-using situation immediately.

Coal-mining

Questions	Resource	Source	Skills
How was coal formed?	text and reference books	library museum	Indexing, scanning, interpretation of diagrams, summarizing
What is coal used for?	charts, tables, descriptions of processes	library, government departments, Coal Board, Electricity Board, Gas Board	Interpretation and collation of information
What are miners like?	interviews, union records, song books, films, history and sociological texts	miners union, libraries	Transposing spoken into written language, reading between lines, evaluating different viewpoints

The ideas contained in this paper are discussed at greater length and with more practical illustrations in Merritt (1973), Farnes (1973) and Moyle (1973).

References

CLYMER, T. (1972) 'What is reading?' in J. E. Merritt and A. Melnik (Eds) *Reading: Today and Tomorrow* London: University of London Press

FARNES, N. (1973) *Reading Purposes, Comprehension and the Use of Context* Milton Keynes: Open University Press

FARNES, N. and MELNIK, A. (1972) Unpublished discussions at the Open University

MERRITT, J. E. (1971) *Reading and the Curriculum* London: Ward Lock Educational

MERRITT, J. E. (1973) *Perspectives on Reading* Milton Keynes: Open University Press

MERRITT, J. E. and MOYLE, D. (1972) Unpublished discussions at the Open University

MOYLE, D. (1970) 'Steps towards structural reading' in *Structure* Henley: Science Research Associates

MOYLE, D. (1973) *The Reading Curriculum* Milton Keynes: Open University Press

PARKER, D. H. (1964) *Schooling for Individual Excellence* New York: Nelson

RUSSELL, D. H. (1961) *Continuity in the Reading Program in Development in and through Reading NSSE* Chicago: University of Chicago Press

STRANG, R. (1972) 'Sequential aspects of reading development' in J. E. Merritt and A. Melnik (Eds) *Reading: Today and Tomorrow* London: University of London Press

12 The work and value of an LEA reading centre

Gerald Platt

Introduction

As in a business venture, a demand creates a service. A need for something more than the Manchester Remedial Service could offer in its present form in the mid 1960s was felt by the heads, teachers, and the inspectorate. An investigation into literacy standards in the city, instigated by the chief inspector, had shown cause for concern. After consultations between senior inspectors and the Remedial Service, three centres for in-service training in the teaching of reading were created, a year later to be increased to four. Although originally intended to exist for only a year or two, the centres are now well established and will no doubt continue as long as such a service is needed.

Comparisons in research

Although the short-term effects of remedial education seem satisfactory, much research has shown the inadequacy of such work in the long term. Perhaps this could be the result of lack of support facilities for the peripatetic remedial teacher in the visited schools. A link needs to be formed between the classteacher and the work of the remedial teacher. The classteacher needs to be trained in remedial work to be able to facilitate a continuous remedial programme for the children inbetween the visits of the remedial teacher. The reading centres were established to forge such links.

Research into the effects of in-service training in the teaching of reading is sparse, but what there is provides for optimistic speculation. Dissatisfaction has been found amongst primary teachers (Goodacre 1970) concerning their opinions of their initial training in the teaching of reading. Similar evidence was provided by Cortis and Dean (1972) and in 1970, Goodacre drew a clear picture of what teachers wanted as far as in-service courses in the teaching of reading was concerned. Chazan (1968) followed up the effects of a diploma course, which included the teaching of reading, and recorded a certain amount of satisfaction felt by the participating teachers in approval of the course as far as suiting them for their jobs was concerned. In America, De Carla and Cleland (1968) described an attempt to determine the effects of in-service training upon classroom behaviour and attitudes of participating teachers and also upon the reading skills and attitudes of their pupils. These writers reported no significant differences in attitude of the teachers as compared with the nonparticipating group. Behavioural changes, concerning teaching procedures, techniques in teaching and beliefs about the teaching of reading, seems to be more affected by the in-service training. Although there did not seem to be any statistical difference between the reading attainments of the experimental and the control groups' pupils, there was indication that the trained teachers' pupils had caught up to the control groups', having started initially at a deficit. Pupils' attitudes did not seem to change significantly although certain dependent variables were affected.

Again from America, Heilman (1965) studied the effects of in-service training on classroom behaviour and reading attainment. Heilman discovered no significant differences in reading scores of the pupils of those teachers who participated on the programme, although there were definite indications that the experimental teachers' pupils had benefitted the most. It was felt, however, that teachers were helped in many ways and that there was evidence that changes in philosophy of the teachers, in their use of new techniques and their attitudes towards their children, would continue to be enhanced as a result of attendance on the programme.

However, Southgate (1967) had cautioned any researcher to be very careful when assessing cause and effect research. Other variables, not directly concerned with the research, may not be easy to control but may create a Hawthorne effect.

It would seem, therefore, that by creating such in-service training in Manchester, the Remedial Service was launching a project on what were not entirely uncharted waters, but which provided some basis for optimism.

Work of the centres

Although labelled 'reading centres', their courses are concerned with a wide remedial educational curriculum, focussed on the teaching of reading. Such training exists mainly for primary school teachers; twelve teachers from twelve schools meet at the four centres for four mornings a week, for four weeks. To facilitate such organization, the LEA provides each participating school with a part-time replacement teacher who stays on at the school for the duration of the course. With some large schools the staffs may be attending the course for over two years, each teacher following his predecessor, until all the staff have been trained. In many EPA schools, where the turnover of staffs is great, a perpetual in-service training programme may well be in operation.

The curriculum of the courses is concerned with preschool learning, pre- and postreading skills, testing procedures, teaching methods, classroom organization, amongst other more general topics. The four heads of the centres are senior teachers in the Remedial Service. As well as running the reading centres, they also each have responsibility for a remedial centre staffed by peripatetic remedial teachers. The heads of the centres, therefore, have to manipulate the machinery which operates on one hand with the teachers attending courses receiving verbal advice etc, and must also help the remedial teachers in their supporting role, to give practical advice etc, in the classroom.

As the teachers who attend a centre usually arrive from those schools which lie within the centre heads' remedial boundaries, all the peripatetic remedial teachers within the same boundaries are also very familiar with the schools. Therefore, the staffs attending the courses receive a continuous in-service programme, whereby they are trained in the mornings and receive follow-up support in the afternoons. The centre heads carry out a large part of the advisory work themselves. They also place in schools reading material such as reading schemes, apparatus, and work books. Some courses are also organized for secondary school teachers on remedial techniques, and as well as helping participating schools, the centres act as resources centres and many visitors from all over the country have been attracted to them.

Value

Probably the best judges of the value of the Manchester centres are those schools which have received training. However, it is also important that the administrators of the centres should evaluate their own worth. Such worth is, however, difficult to measure. It is certain that the courses are valued very highly because, what was first envisaged as a one-year experiment is still after four years continuing and developing. It is suspected, though, that the centres' effectiveness, as measured by careful research, is complicated by what, as Southgate warns, is a very fluctuating complex problem.

I am, at present, evaluating the effects of the Manchester centres. A piece of research which had done this previously, but on a much smaller scale, was conducted by Brannen (1971), who reported a definite gain in reading scores in favour of 'trained' teachers' children, although not in attitude scores. The purpose of the present study (Platt 1974) is to examine the possible effects of the in-service training in three of the four Manchester reading centres, viewed according to:

1   the differences in effects between experimental (trained) and controlled groups, i.e. treatment
2   which centre the 'trained' teachers attended, i.e. area
3   the amount of backwardness in reading witnessed in the schools, i.e. need
4   differences in effects between boys and girls in the sample, i.e. sex
5   the differences in scores tested immediately before training, immediately after, and some six months later.

Thirty-six first-year junior teachers were concerned in the experiment. Eighteen teachers chosen at random who had attended courses made up the experimental group. Another random sample of eighteen control teachers, who resembled the 'trained' teachers in that they were also first-year junior class teachers, taught in similar schools which represented similar needs, were chosen but did not attend courses. The effects of the experiment were observed through the following measures:

1 reading tests results
2 children's measured attitudes to reading results
3 teachers' ratings of their children as readers
4 teachers' measured attitudes to teaching reading
5 inventory questionnaire results on classroom teaching practices
6 autobiographical data on each teacher.

Other variables such as IQ and attendances of the classes were also observed. The collected data is at the moment being analysed by means of five-way analysis of variance. Although such analysis is as yet incomplete, the indications are that it supports Brannen's findings. Children's reading attainment, as measured by group tests of comprehension and word recognition, does seem to be affected by whether their teachers have attended an in-service training programme. Children's attitudes to reading also seem to be affected but apparently not their teachers' attitudes to teaching them. However, without far more scrutiny of the apparent results, findings can only be speculative.

Research, for example, into attitude testing has shown this to be a very difficult area and one which is not free from subjectivity. Also, as Southgate (1967) warns, the problem of a 'reading-drive' could have been still apparent in this study, although measures were taken to suppress such effects.

Conclusions

What is evident to me, after organizing in-service courses in the teaching of reading for some years, is that there is a perpetual demand from heads and teachers for extra training in teaching reading. Such demand is not necessarily a direct criticism of initial training—many teachers need a backcloth of experience to appreciate both theory and practical lectures. What is necessary, however, is that such in-service training is administered, not by lecturers, but by practising teachers *who can daily mix with teachers in the classroom.* Advisory supporting activity is a necessary corollary to in-service education. The lecturer must be able to relate his lectures directly to immediate personal experience. As a remedial teacher, I find that remedial experience with small groups of children is not extremely useful, and I have to gain current experience, day by day, working with teachers in the classroom.

What is also evident is that infant and special school teachers need such training and are not, just because of their status, any more efficient or more highly trained to teach reading than their junior counterparts.

Also, as a personal view, it seems that both teaching practical methodology and theory to teachers is no long lasting answer. What has to come about is a cementing together in better rapport of the isolated nursery, infant, junior institutions. Heads and staffs of separate schools have to communicate and pass on information. Teachers, even in their own staffrooms, have to mix professionally, and hopefully, socially with their own colleagues. Not only do such teachers have to like children, they also have to like teachers. In this way the best atmosphere in which to learn will be fostered for *both* teachers and children.

References

BRANNEN, B. (1971) *The evaluation of an in-service course for teachers in the teaching of reading* Unpublished Diploma in Educational Guidance Dissertation, Manchester University

CHAZAN, M. (1968) A follow-up survey of mature students *University College of Swansea Journal* 27-29

CORTIS, G. A. and DEAN, A. J. (1972) Teaching skills of probationary primary school teachers: a follow-up survey *Educational Research* 13, 3

DE CARLA, M. R. and CLELAND, D. L. (1968) A reading in-service educational program for teachers *The Reading Teacher* 165-167

GOODACRE, E. J. (1970) What the teachers want *Times Educational Supplement* 27th November

HEILMAN, A. W. (1965) Effects of an intensive in-service programme on teachers' classroom behaviour and pupils' reading achievement *Cooperative Research Project No. 2709* Pennsylvania: Pennsylvania State University

PLATT, G. F. *The effects of in-service training on the teaching of reading* Proposed MEd thesis, Manchester University

13 Training the teachers of reading for the junior/middle school

Christopher Walker

A period of growth reviewed

This year's UKRA presidential address was entitled 'The teaching of reading—a crisis?' Crisis and the accompanying question mark are not unknown to those of us who have been involved with training personnel to teach reading in recent years. We were aware, long before the Start and Wells enquiry, that reading standards were unnecessarily low and we can take credit for not awaiting the findings of the Bullock Commission to improve the quality of teacher training in this field. The last six years have seen considerable expansion in the colleges of staffing, courses, time and resources devoted to the teaching of reading. In-service courses have mushroomed. The annual one-term in-service course 'Reading and language in the primary school' at Mather College has now completed its fifth year and an additional one-term course in reading development is planned for 1975. Donald Moyle at Edge Hill has just completed his third successive diploma course; William Latham has just finished the first diploma course at Sheffield; and Derek Thackray is to start a diploma course at Rugby next month. Chorley College has just completed its pilot course (a six week intensive retraining) for the heads of local schools and is about to embark on the retraining by half-term courses of the staffs of all primary schools in the area. In 1974 Tony Robinson at Shenstone is to start a one-term in-service course in the teaching of reading. Outside the colleges, but often working in conjunction with them, some 300 teachers centres, many of which incorporate reading centres, offer courses varying from day release to one month in the teaching of reading. Many college of education personnel make notable contributions to teachers centre activity.

At initial training level, growth in the teaching of reading has been phenomenal, despite the difficulties occasioned in the last six years by the need to double the output of the nation's teachers and to provide both graduate and postgraduate courses for many of them. The colleges have served the nation well and in the space of five or six years have ended a teacher shortage which has been endemic since the war. This has been done by the difficult expedient of box and cox.

Staffing problems

That there should be growth in the teaching of reading at all is almost miraculous in that until recently there has been no high-level qualification in this specialism and therefore no cadre of recognized experts from which the colleges might draw. The reading tutors in the colleges are drawn either from education or English departments, chiefly the former, and as education tutors the colleges invest them with the principal task of tutoring education groups in psychology, sociology, the history of education, philosophy and in preparing them for, and supervising them in, teaching practice. Despite this multiplicity of roles, many education tutors have considerably augmented both the content and the time devoted to training in the teaching of reading. My own college is typical of many in this respect. In 1967 the time devoted to the teaching of reading amounted to six hours in a three years course. In 1973 in the same college every student has a sixty-five hour course in the teaching of reading.

Changes in course orientation

The emphasis has also altered dramatically. Some five or six years ago the only students with any worthwhile training in the teaching of reading were those preparing to teach infants. Junior trainees got little more than a few tips in remedial teaching, i.e. beginning reading for older children.

The current view, which is rapidly gaining ground in the colleges, is that the teacher of reading in junior/middle schools needs a much longer training than the infant teacher, who is basically concerned only with beginning reading. The junior/middle school teacher must be prepared to teach reading at three levels:

1 At beginning level, for the 45 per cent of children who are still not beyond Book 3 of the infant primer on transfer to junior school. For these pupils infant methods must continue.
2 At remedial level for some. It is necessary here to distinguish between the corrective treatment which certain children require and the more long-term, carefully structured programmes suitable for those of slow developmental pattern.
3 At extension level for the majority as they achieve basic competence in their progress through the middle years of schooling.

A college course outlined

Such a view of the role of junior/middle school staff in teaching reading necessitates training in beginning reading which is at least as extensive as that which infant personnel normally receive. In my own college this starts with a thorough theoretical basis to which all subsequent practice can be related. In their introduction to the psychology of reading, students are led by models and simulations to study reading both as a set of intricate mental processes and as a system of communication. The many factors—physical, social, emotional and intellectual—which affect the child's ability to read are also studied, as are important aspects of reading matter such as the principles affecting legibility and readability. The prereading element in the course deals practically with techniques and materials designed to develop both visual and auditory discrimination and to develop oral language facility, including listening, by direct and vicarious experiences. The whole gamut of established readiness procedures is summarized in a prereading record which enables students to observe and record individual child growth towards reading by incorporating the widest possible range of indicators. The formal beginnings of reading introduce look and say, phonic and eclectic approaches via schemes and materials which exemplify these respectively. The phonic element is extremely thorough and requires at least fifteen hours. Of these, five are direct contact time devoted to analysing the most important phonic stages and progressions and to the description, handling and organization of games and apparatus suitable at each stage. The other ten hours are practical time when students, under supervision, begin to make the teaching kit which enables them to teach the various stages of phonics. Over a period of two years the kit becomes a comprehensive set of practical teaching aids. Work is also done on story methods and language experience approaches, and on teacher-prepared reading materials associated with project work. There is ample exemplifying material of the latter category devised by students in previous years. In our teaching practice zone there is much experimentation with minority methods such as ita and various colour-cuing systems. As it is possible in one of three teaching practices to encounter such approaches, it is felt that the students value the versatility they derive from the teachers' course in reading and writing ita and from some instruction in Gattegno's *Words in Colour*. Finally, the beginning stage part of the student assignment includes the evaluation of two reading schemes which exemplify quite different pedagogical and psychological standpoints.

At extension level students are introduced to multilevel and programmed approaches such as SRA *Reading Laboratories* and Ward Lock Educational *Reading Workshops* and are also encouraged to programme their own reading assignments for children on simple linear teaching machines. Study skills are geared to SQ3R activities at the students' own level, as are exercises in speed reading, fluency and anticipation training. Critical reading is developed by oral discussion group approaches based on silent reading, also at student level. How to foster the reading habit is treated practically by the discussion of case studies in the use of reading interviews and inventories. The principles of teaching remedial reading and the treatment of slow learners are derived from discussion of case studies which exemplify good practice. This involves some instruction in diagnostic testing and treatment. Readability assessment both by cloze procedure and the use of Fry's Readability Graph is done practically by student participation using a variety of children's texts.

The course is conducted by lectures over a period of two years, but although a considerable amount of demonstration and direct teaching is given, the onus is put squarely on the students to be responsible for their own learning. This is done by requiring each student to produce a reading file in which lecture notes are expanded, abstracts from the literature inserted, and all experience acquired on teaching practice and in other situations, e.g. weekly school visits, is documented. Incorporated in the reading file are the phonic teaching kit and reading games and apparatus made for specific teaching assignments.

The above outline indicates how one college has extended its reading course over a period of six years. Similar developments have taken place in other colleges and, although I know of no tutor who is satisfied with either the content or the time allotted to teaching reading, there is no doubt that considerable interest and expertise have grown up in the training field over the past few years.

Changes in school systems

There is need for continued improvement in training programmes to equip teachers to teach reading with the versatility and sophistication which rapidly changing school systems require. One cannot prepare students for every possible eventuality, but things are less simple than they were when the middle years meant juniors and they were children between seven and eleven years old. At the present time, in the conurbation served by my college the largest authority has retained its junior schools but adjacent divisions have middle schools for children between eight and twelve in one area, between nine and thirteen in another, and one LEA has middle schools for children between ten and thirteen. Such an age spread (seven to thirteen) makes training for the middle years a complex task compared with the training of infant teachers. Additional complications from the point of view of teaching reading are imposed by the almost universal trend towards open plan schools. Their designers have yet to come up with solutions to excessive noises and distraction, the very conditions which most frustrate attempts to teach reading effectively.

Changes in the structure of higher education

This conference has seen much concern expressed about the implications for the teaching of reading of the James Report and the White Paper on Higher Education. Though the possibility of improved in-service training provision is universally welcomed, the likelihood of initial training being reduced from three years to one has few supporters. Professional training will become for all the crash course which is at present confined to post-graduates. I know of no one concerned with postgraduate training who finds it in any way comparable either in quality or quantity with that given to three-year trained certificate or four-year trained BEd students. In my own college the maximum time that can be allotted to postgraduates for the teaching of reading is little more than half of that available to other student categories. In the same college, the postgraduate reading files produced after one year are very inferior to those of the certificate and BEd students who have had three years to study, practice and conceptualize their knowledge and experience. In-service training would indeed be an absolute necessity if one year professional training were the rule, but to increase in-service provision only by sacrificing the very substantial progress that the recent past has seen in initial training would appear to me to be a retrograde step. Once again, until their period of secondment came around (seven years?)—and not all teachers would opt to study reading on secondment—we would be sending into schools teachers ill-equipped to teach reading. They would be forced, like teachers of my generation were, to learn by trial and error at great cost to themselves and the children at whose expense their painfully acquired expertise would be developed. The tidying-up of the administrative structure of higher education need not be done by forcing upon the colleges a system which would result in our sending into schools teachers unable to teach literacy with any confidence or sophistication.

A personal view

My own solution for improved professional training would be to begin a four-year training for all as soon as possible. The Secretary of State for Education assures us that we now have a surplus of teachers so no harm would be done if for one year no new teachers left college to take up first appointments in school. Four years training would surely be worth graduate status, especially if the extra year were devoted to dramatically improving the quality of professional, as opposed to academic, training. In this context the time devoted to the teaching of reading could be universally augmented to, say, the ninety hours which American teachers usually receive as a minimum, and this should be compulsory for all who seek a teaching qualification. In addition, there is a great need to train reading specialists at every level and this could be done by allowing those students sufficiently qualified and motivated to take a four-year main course in the teaching of reading to graduate level. To operate such courses reading tutors need to be liberated from the manifold demands imposed on them by education departments and the setting up of reading departments in the training institutions needs to be facilitated. If reading as a subject had such status there would surely not be for long in 'the teaching of reading—a crisis!'

Day 3
Convenor: Tony Pugh

14 The development of silent reading

Tony Pugh

Introduction

Silent reading is a modern activity. Reading silently was almost unknown
to the scholars of the classical and medieval worlds (Chaytor 1945), while
during the Renaissance the term 'reading' undoubtedly connoted oral reading (Mathews 1966). Only during the nineteenth century does silent reading become commonplace for, as Chaytor comments, the British Museum
reading-room would be intolerably noisy if it were filled with the buzz of
whispering and muttering which accompanied reading in the Middle Ages.

One should beware, however, of assuming that silent reading came about
simply because reading aloud is a distraction to others. The medieval monks
led an almost completely communal life, yet they had to be isolated in
carrels when they engaged in reading. Examination of factors related to
the historical development of silent reading reveals that it became the usual
and optimum mode of reading for most adult reading tasks mainly because
the tasks themselves changed in character.

The change in the tasks demanded that a mode of reading be developed
which was not only nonoral but which also had its own distinctive qualities
and applications. It is the purpose of this paper to examine why silent
reading is now so widespread and to point to the skills and attitudes
required by the effective silent reader. It will then be possible to judge to
what extent research and teaching has taken account of these skills and
attitudes.

Historical factors related to the growth of silent reading

The last century saw a steady gradual increase in literacy (Cipolla 1969),
and thus in the number of readers. As readers increased so the number of
potential listeners declined, and thus there was some reduction in the need
to read aloud. As reading for the benefit of listeners grew less common so
came the flourishing of reading as a private activity in such public places as
libraries, railway carriages and offices where reading aloud would cause
distraction to other readers.

More important, however, than the factors mentioned so far is the
change in the volume and in the application of what was read. Newspapers
were read avidly, so much so that by 1850 Richard Cobden (cited Webb
1958) claimed that a busy man had little time to read anything other than
periodical literature; furthermore he doubted whether one could better
employ the limited time available for reading, and distrusted those who

liked it to be thought that they read whole books.

Those who did wish to be thought well read were resisting the compartmentalization of knowledge which came in Victorian England and were holding to the aristocratic and nonspecialized culture which was rapidly being eroded. The reading of fiction, especially serious social commentary, declined in relative importance during the century at the same time as public libraries grew very rapidly to cater for private reading for specialized information. Interestingly the reading of light fiction was a lower middle-class pursuit after the 1850 Library Act, whereas it was the artisans who borrowed the solid books (Webb 1958).

The use of books for self-improvement through learning was well established by the middle of the century. Employers often encouraged it, so much so that as early as the 1820s the rent of a village inn owned by the London Lead Company was regularly reduced, 'the miners preferring books to drink' (Raistrick and Jennings 1965).

Towards the end of the century there was still considerable argument over whether books should be used for information or treated respectfully, and over whether the reading of ephemeral material such as newspapers was in some way mentally debilitating. Indeed the argument remains with us still in education. However, whatever its virtues, the old shared literary culture had gone, and was replaced by the printed mass media and by books and periodicals for a specialized readership.

In 1887, A. J. Balfour gave a rectorial address to the students of St Andrews University entitled 'The pleasures of reading' (Balfour 1888). He attacked very strongly those who held that only great books should be read and that they should be read with some deference to their authors. He parodied those readers who ask for a reading scheme of 'great books' and then read so that their only desire is to finish the book and their only reward is self-denial. Balfour felt it necessary to stress that skipping sections of a book is not cheating, and he asserted that 'he has only half learnt the art of reading who has not added to it the more refined accomplishments of skipping and skimming'.

Thus by the end of the century students were being recommended to adopt attitudes to books and to use skills in reading them which were inappropriate, if not impossible, for the oral reader. The social, cultural and technological changes in the century had greatly altered what the term reading connoted.

The advantages of silent reading

The proliferation of mass media in this century has not made reading obsolete but it has helped to clarify its special advantages. Any reader has certain advantages over the nonreader. He has access to an extremely wide range of information which is conveniently available at most times and in most places. He has no need for playback devices (as in a sense he is one) nor is he at the mercy of programme schedules or programme planners. He may, either mentally or by making notes, store the information he receives in the code in which it was originally stored and is thus under no obligation to translate from one code to another (unlike, for example, a listener to a symphony who cannot fully reproduce the original 'message').

However, the view of a reader as a playback device or a mere receptor for other men's words is somewhat limiting, for the true silent reader has not only the advantages mentioned but many others which are denied to those whose model of reading is based on oral reading. Perhaps the most fundamental advantage is that the reading of the effective silent reader is self-paced; thus he can vary his attention and speed, and interrupt his reading, according to his needs. In drawing attention to this behaviour in the effective reader, Morris (1963) shows that McLuhanites who regard reading as a linear, sequential process display a limited understanding of what reading can involve. However, not only is the reader self-paced but he is also able to use a book as 'a machine to think with' (Richards 1924). He is not, therefore, directed exclusively by the author; he is able rather to decide for himself, in the light of his purposes and priorities, how to treat what an author has to offer.

Skills used in silent reading

Understanding what can be done in silent reading may change a reader's attitude to texts but it need not, in itself, produce a change in performance. It is useful, therefore, to examine some of the skills used in silent reading, their applications and their distinguishing visual behaviour.

The list given below is based on observing readers whose purpose is known and who are effective in attaining their purpose. It will be noted that the reader changes his visual behaviour according to his purpose and that the more exactly definable the purpose, the more rapid the reading. It is not, however, implied that in the course of a single reading of any text a reader will use one of the skills exclusively, for he may modify his purpose in the light of what an author has to offer.

Skill	*Application to a text*	*Observable visual behaviour*
Scanning	Locating a predetermined symbol or group of symbols (e.g. word, phrase, formula, date).	Very rapid inspection and occasional close inspection of text. The linearity of the text is not followed nor often is the overall sequence of the text. Backward and forward movement within the text is common.
Search reading	Locating information on a predetermined topic when the precise symbolic representation is not known.	Rapid inspection, punctuated by short periods (varying in duration) of closer inspection of the text. There is some tendency to observe the overall sequence though not the linearity of the text.

Skill	Application to a text	Observable visual behaviour
		Backward and forward movement within the text is common.
Skimming	(i) Deciding whether to make use of a text. (ii) Deciding how to approach a text. (iii) Obtaining for its own sake an overall impression of certain features of a text (e.g. surface information, structure, tone). (iv) Obtaining advance organization of a text which has to be known but which presents difficulties. (v) Reviewing after reading for checking or clarification.	Rate of inspection and degree of attention are very varied. The overall sequence of the text is usually followed though not its linearity. Backward and forward movement (*especially* within a double page) is very common.
Receptive reading	Discovering accurately what an author conveys.	Linear and sequential movement through the text is usual, though accompanied by some occasional references back. Extremely close attention to the visual task is typical.
Responsive reading	Using what an author conveys as a prompt to reflective, relational or creative thinking.	Linear and sequential movement through the text is usual, accompanied by some reference back. Extremely close attention to the text interspersed with periods (of varying duration) where there is no visual attention is typical.

Definitions of reading

The kinds of reading behaviour given involve the use of a strategic approach to achieving a goal. The strategy adopted will often require the reader to fail deliberately to observe certain conventions which the writer has followed, and which are appropriate for those whose model of reading is based on oral reading.

It may now be rare to find subscribers to a definition of reading based solely on phonic reproduction of graphic symbols (Downing 1972). Even so it is disturbing to note that it is rarely made explicit that Thorndike's reading as reasoning (Thorndike 1917) or Goodman's psycholinguistic guessing game (Goodman 1967) both involve the uses of approaches which are inappropriate to linear oral reading. It is silent reading which permits the varying degree of attention to parts of a text and the constant reference back which generally accepted definitions of reading assume.

Regrettably the search for an elegant definition of reading blurs the the varieties of behaviour and certain writers have failed even to make a clear distinction between silent reading and oral reading. Thus doubtful inferences are sometimes made from one mode of reading to the other. For example Weber (1968), reviewing the literature on miscues, remarks on the dangers of drawing conclusions about cues used in silent reading from errors made in oral reading. Similarly, Marchbanks and Levin (1965), in their discussion of word recognition theories, warn of the dangers of generalizing to children in a classroom from evidence collected from mature adult readers reading under rather specialized conditions imposed by tachistoscopic experiments.

Research into silent reading

One of the reasons for low awareness of the varied characteristics of silent reading is to be found, oddly enough, in the model of silent reading implied in the extensive early research in the area and in the educational developments which followed. Thus, although there is a large body of reputable research, its effects are in some ways unfortunate. This is particularly to be regretted in view of the fact that silent reading attracted the attention of psychological researchers at a time when the assessment of the merits of the various approaches to beginning reading was based almost exclusively on opinion.

It is inappropriate to give a full account of the many researches undertaken between about 1880 and 1930. The interested reader is referred to Huey (1908), Vernon (1931), Carmichael and Dearborn (1948), Anderson and Dearborn (1952), and Tinker (1965), and to a thorough review of the literature on subvocalization given by Conrad (1972). It must suffice to remark here that all the early experimental researches concentrated upon either the visual perception of small units or upon sequential thorough reading of a text. Thus in the tachistoscopic experiments the concern was with words, phrases, and groups of letters or digits; while in the experiments to record eye movements the mode of reading was more akin to silent oral reading than to true silent reading. These remarks should not be taken as necessarily implying criticism of the researchers. Often their aim was 'to completely analyse what we do when we read . . . (so as) to describe very many of the most intricate workings of the human mind' (Huey 1908) and the more mundane matter of improving silent reading ability had low priority.

Unfortunately major conclusions were drawn about means of improving reading which the evidence would not support. It was found that 'good readers' tended to have a wide eye-span, to spend less time in regressive eye-movements, to spend less time per fixation and to make fewer obvious lip movements. Here the evidence is convincing provided that it is used descriptively. However, the common mistake tended to be that of assuming that causal relationships existed when they had not in fact been established. Thus one still often finds dubious assumptions about causality in reading textbooks, in speed reading courses and in the rationale for certain reading machines (see Pugh 1972a).

The view held was that attack on the symptoms of poor reading would help to overcome the causes of poor reading performance. In fact, a careful examination of the literature strongly suggests that the major factor which effected change in reading speed was motivated practice in reading quickly. O'Brien (1921) relates that many of the researchers of the period, himself included, had increased their speed of reading by no more complex a method than willing themselves to do so; the similarity in results between O'Brien's experimental groups serves further to support this view that the common factor causing increased reading speed among the schoolchildren studied was their willingness to comply to the expectation that they would read more quickly.

One factor to which O'Brien did pay some attention was the role of purpose in reading and he obtained records of eye-movements which showed that speed of reading varied with the type and density of questions to be asked after reading. O'Brien seems to have put this finding to little practical use but West (1926), working in Bengal, devised a course which relied heavily on varying question density so that his pupils would learn a variety of reading speeds for various purposes.

West's book is particularly interesting for its discussion of the aims of teaching silent reading in his particular context, and for its careful examination of the validity of the exercises he used in attempting to achieve these aims. Perhaps it was the situation obtaining in Bengal at that time which led him to doubt the value of exercises which required the pupil to 'just read' and then answer some unseen questions. Certainly West was acutely aware of the importance of transfer of learning, or the cash-in value of an education, as he called it, and such awareness caused him to assess achievement in school exercises against the criterion of ability to perform real-life tasks.

Possibly the postponement, by formal education, of real-life tasks in the developed countries, taken with the elegance of the research methods, caused so much dubious generalization from the eye-movement research mentioned to reading outside the research situation. Whatever the reason, it is still not generally realized that there are severe limitations in an approach to improving silent reading which does no more than try to increase speed in sequential reading tasks. Thus Hodgins (1961) reports that the speed reading films for pacing formed the basis for remedial reading courses at Harvard for a number of years before it was found that the techniques developed had little transfer value. Students who could read more quickly were reluctant to use a strategic approach to reading even when such an approach had obvious merits. I would go even further and suggest that regular practice in rapid sequential reading may of itself preclude the student's use of an appropriate approach to certain tasks simply because of the mental set induced by the exercises used in the course.

Research techniques for studying realistic silent reading tasks

If early research methodology and speed reading courses, which owed as much to the methodology as to the findings of that research, are both of dubious value, then it is necessary to devise research and teaching procedures which relate to a less limited type of reading behaviour than that described in the last section.

Two research methods are worthy of note in this connection. A method devised at Brunel University (see Thomas and Augstein 1972), uses continuous stationary text which is read through a window. The text can be wound either backwards or forwards or, of course, held still. A recording facility is incorporated so that the investigator can discover at what point and for how long the subject has dwelt on a part of the text, where he has gone back in the text and so on. The recorder provides gross measurement of reading behaviour in complete texts but the method has the disadvantage that the subject is not reading in book format.

To overcome this difficulty apparatus has been devised by myself (Pugh 1972b) at the University of Leeds. The method adopted was suggested by the Purdue eye-camera (Karslake 1940) which was developed to record attention to advertising copy. The copy was read through a semisilvered mirror and a reflected image of the subject's head, superimposed on a direct image of the copy, was photographed on motion film. However, it has been found that it is very difficult to read book text through a semi-silvered mirror. Thus, although this type of mirror is retained, its purpose is to avoid distracting the reader, to whom, owing to the angle and lighting of the mirror, it appears as a piece of glass. This 'glass' forms the top half of a reading stand, the book being placed on the lower half. A direct image of the book and an indirect image of the subject's head are recorded on video-tape and the method has proved useful for observing and recording how a subject approaches specified reading tasks in ordinary books. The disadvantage of the method is that it produces no print-out of results and thus is time consuming for the investigator who must keep notes and make certain judgments.

Secondary schools and silent reading

If reading now connotes silent reading to most adults in this country, it is unlikely that it has this connotation for most children. Even in secondary education oral reading is commonplace and, at least in the teaching of English, many teachers consider that it should be so (Calthrop 1971). The question arises, however, as to whether schools' use of oral reading as the mode of reading (with literature often the medium) is a sound practice or whether the practice is outdated and hard to justify. Whichever is the case there are good grounds for thinking that reading methods and approaches to reading in secondary education have neither attraction for the pupil

116

(Pugh 1971) nor any direct relevance to the needs of the adult reader.

Schools, however, are faced with a dilemma. By their very organizational nature they are obliged to involve groups of children in shared activities, yet they must also prepare children for eventual autonomous learning. Attempts to foster skills and interests necessary for private learning would seem unlikely to be of much avail, if autonomous work is rarely done in the schools.

Apart from such curricular considerations one must also take into account the fact that there may, in any case, be dangers in dispensing with oral reading. There are grounds for arguing that aural cues can be valuable in developing reading fluency at certain stages (as Daly argues in chapter 15), and a method based on aural cues has been found to be useful in helping foreign students to read fluently in English (Neville and Pugh 1973). It should be noted, perhaps, that the recorded aural cues referred to by these writers are probably more helpful for the reader than those supplied by a fellow pupil reading an unprepared text.

Although such aural cueing may develop fluency it does not of itself promote true silent reading and it would be too simple to assert that secondary schools should use silent reading as the sole mode of reading, taking as justification the fact that adults rarely read aloud. Such justification led to the attempt, reported by Buswell (1945), to teach Chicago first and second graders to begin reading by entirely nonoral methods. The results of the ten year experiment are not convincing but this extreme case may serve to draw attention to the dangers inherent in the tendency to assert that the effective adult reader provides a useful model for children. The concept of a model adult reader is only useful if it is firmly realized that he is a model of what children should attain and not a model to be copied. The illiterate is adept at copying the visual behaviour of the effective adult reader; the skills which an illiterate must gain and subsume in order to really read like the model are still far from clear.

Conclusion

The road to effective reading is certainly not as direct as the Chicago experiment assumed. It is more likely that it traverses a number of stages and Goodman (1968) proposes a convenient model in which reading development is seen as having three stages which are related to the oral, aural and silent modes.

This paper has been concerned with the silent mode and with stressing the need for a differentiation between true silent reading, which involves a wide variety of goal-directed skills, and the aural stage (or reading fluency) which involves rapid sequential 'listening in' to a text. Clearly both this aural stage and the earlier oral stage are prerequisites for effective adult silent reading. Such reading, however, requires the use of skills inappropriate to oral and aural reading. A description of these skills was offered earlier: much fuller discussion on how these skills might be assessed and developed is now needed.

References

ANDERSON, I. H. and DEARBORN, W. F. (1952) *The Psychology of Teaching Reading* New York: Ronald Press

BALFOUR, A. J. (1888) *The Pleasures of Reading* Edinburgh: Blackwood

BUSWELL, G. T. (1945) *Nonoral Reading—A Study of its Use in the Chicago Public Schools* (Supplementary Educational Monograph 60) Chicago: University of Chicago Press

CALTHROP, K. (1971) *Reading Together—An Investigation into the Use of the Class Reader* London: Heinemann

CARMICHAEL, L. and DEARBORN, H. J. (1945) *From Script to Print—An Introduction to Medieval Vernacular Literature* Cambridge: Heffer

CIPOLLA, C. M. (1969) *Literacy and Development in the West* Harmondsworth: Penguin

CONRAD, R. (1972) 'Speech and reading' in J. F. Kavanagh and I. G. Mattingly (Eds) *Language by Ear and by Eye* Cambridge, Mass.: MIT Press

DOWNING, J. (1972) The meaning of 'reading' *Reading* 6, 3

GOODMAN, K. S. (1967) Reading: a psycholinguistic guessing game *Journal of the Reading Specialist* 6, 126-135

GOODMAN, K. S. (1968) 'The psycholinguistic nature of the reading process' in K. S. Goodman (Ed) *The Psycholinguistic Nature of the Reading Process* Detroit: Wayne University Press

HODGINS, R. C. (1961) 'The text is the adversary' in G. B. Blaine Jnr. and C. C. McArthur (Eds) *Emotional Problems of the Student* New York: Appleton-Century-Crofts

HUEY, E. B. (1908) *The Psychology and Pedagogy of Reading* New York: Macmillan (reprinted MIT Press, 1968)

KARSLAKE, J. S. (1940) The Purdue eye-camera: a practical apparatus for studying the attention value of advertisements *Journal of Applied Psychology* 24, 417-440

MARCHBANKS, G. and LEVIN, H. (1965) Cues by which children recognize words *Journal of Educational Psychology* 56, 2, 57-61

MATHEWS, M. M. (1966) *Teaching to Read—Historically Considered* Chicago: University of Chicago Press

MORRIS, R. (1963) *Success and Failure in Learning to Read* London: Oldbourne

NEVILLE, M. and PUGH, A. K. (1973) An exploratory study of the application of time-compressed and time-expanded speech in the development of the English reading proficiency of foreign students *English Language Teaching* (in press)

O'BRIEN, J. A. (1921) *Silent Reading* New York: Macmillan

PUGH, A. K. (1971) 'Reading in the secondary school: an unassumed responsibility' in V. Southgate (Ed) *Literacy at All Levels* London: Ward Lock Educational

PUGH, A. K. (1972a) Adult reading: theory and practice *Reading* 6, 3, 23-29

PUGH, A. K. (1972b) *Initial Report on the Experimental Investigation of*

Adult Reading Behaviour using CCTV Equipment (mimeo) Leeds: University of Leeds

RAISTRICK, A. and JENNINGS, B. (1965) *A History of Lead Mining in the Pennines* London: Longman

RICHARDS, I. A. (1924) *Principles of Literary Criticism* London: Routledge and Kegan Paul

THOMAS, L. F. and AUGSTEIN, S. (1972) An experimental approach to the study of reading as a learning skill *Research in Education* 8, 28-46

THORNDIKE, E. L. (1917) Reading as reasoning: a study of mistakes in paragraph reading *Journal of Educational Psychology* 8, 323-332

TINKER, M. A. (1965) *Bases for Effective Reading* Minneapolis: Cambridge University Press

VERNON, M. D. (1931) *The Experimental Study of Reading* Cambridge: Cambridge University Press

WEBB, R. K. (1958) 'The Victorian reading public' in B. Ford (Ed) *From Dickens to Hardy* (Pelican Guide to English Literature 6) Harmonsworth: Penguin

WEBER, R. (1968) The study of oral reading errors: a survey of the literature *Reading Research Quarterly* 4, 96-119

WEST, M. (1926) *Bilingualism* Calcutta: Government of India

15 Developing aural skills with some consideration of their role in developing reading fluency

B. V. Daly

Introduction

The ear is a tremendously sensitive organ; at some sound frequencies the eardrum's vibrations are as small as one billionth of a centimetre (Békésy 1957). In fact, the ear has the largest range of energy sensitivity of any of our sense organs. These two factors are stated at the outset, not only to redress the imbalance in those texts on perception which are generally heavily biased toward material on visual perception, but also to prepare the reader for the emphasis in what is to follow. The eye is not always superior to, or independent of, the ear.

The language arts of reading, writing, listening and speech are certainly related to one another. According to Spearritt's (1962) factorial analyses, listening comprehension and reading comprehension are closely connected, and each appears to be more closely related to the other than to IQ (Wilkinson and Stratta 1970).

One must beware, however, of treating reading as though it were a primary assimilative linguistic skill, as listening indeed is. Most children will not proceed with the same ease in the early stages of learning to read as they did in the early stages of learning to listen. Nor, indeed, is there any formula which guarantees that a child who has reached a particular fluency in oral development will proceed without difficulty in the early stages of learning to read (Martin 1955). This latter point is particularly relevant in assessing the value of those compensatory education programmes and prereading linguistic enrichment schemes which are exclusively oral in content. This may seem an obvious point, but trends towards a more heuristic model of education have brought some startling over-simplifications in the field of language learning. Holt (1967) is a recent exponent of the recurring view that children will 'discover' reading as and when they are ready, provided that the right materials are available. Attractive though this notion is, there are strong counter arguments such as those stated by Southgate (1970). This view is entirely compatible with my experience that some children who have been exposed to a wide range of materials often want to read books but cannot do so for lack of basic guidance in the beginning stages of learning to read.

In discussing the development of aural ability consideration will be given to aural alternatives to the reading of printed matter and to the training of listening skills. The relationship between the development of listening skills and reading skills will also be examined.

Aural reading and visual reading: some parallels and possibilities

Aural reading may be defined as the selection and interpretation of non-conversational verbal communications in the form of spoken words. There appears to be *a priori* evidence that the information processing ability of one who reads by listening is not taxed under normal conditions. In fact, as McLuhan has emphasized, until the advent of print technology man *never* processed language at a rate faster than normal speech. Morris (1963) also noted that print technology has made it possible for the reader to assimilate information not only at a different rate, but also in a different sequence from that which the producer intended. Recent developments in aural technology may well afford a similar degree of flexibility to the aural reader.

The speed of a recorded message may be increased using a speech compressor (Foulke and Sticht 1969) and there is also the possibility of varying the rate of compression continuously by varying pause time at phrase boundaries, a technique reported by Bever (1968). More organization may be built into recorded material by using high speed forward indexing techniques, which according to Foulke (1968) can be superimposed on a recorded compressed message thus facilitating a fast forward scanning procedure which does not interfere with the main message since the vocal pitches of the two messages would be quite different. It would also appear possible to utilize the second track of tape as an indexing track on a specially adapted tape player. The most pertinent aspect of this track would be that it be recorded in reverse at the rewind speed so that certain structural properties of the main track would become apparent during the rewinding process. Efficient forms of indexing tape material could be researched, but it is suggested that time signals or 'paragraph' headings, or simple one line summaries, be tried as indexing techniques for recorded oral material.

When one considers that the aural reader also has the speaker's tone of voice and inflexion to guide an understanding of the message, as well as an indication of the speaker's personality, then there appears to be no theoretical reason why visual reading should, necessarily, be the superior mode of reading for all purposes and for all people.

The information explosion demands selectivity for survival; the flexibility and control the individual has over incoming aural messages depends not only on technical innovation but also on the listening skills the recipient possesses.

Training in listening skills

Having examined some of the technology involved in improving listening media, attention is now given to improving the listener's skills in processing information. After a thorough review of the literature on training in listening skills, Devine (1967) concludes that certain listening skills undoubtedly improve with training. The questions which need to be asked regarding the research and published materials in this field are:

121

1 What particular skills are being trained and how were they isolated?
2 To what situation is the improved listening skill *likely* to relate?

The second question deals with the problem of the transfer of a particular skill to a different situation. Educators must be concerned with transfer. They need to know—or at least to make reasonably informed assumptions about—the degree to which the skill which has been isolated and taught is useful in real situations. Ellis (1965) deals more fully with the question of what is involved in transfer of learning but for the present it is sufficient to assert that the validity of tests of listening abilities must be carefully examined in considering reports on research in this field.

Working at Iowa, Steen (1969) found that auditory memory, in terms of series recall, could be improved by training at the kindergarten stage. This particular finding could have significance to teachers who wish to point out certain phonic regularities in aural language as a prereading activity.

Kennedy and Weener (1973) found that for underachieving readers, training in listening using cloze procedure could be very effective when testing was on a cloze-type listening test. Although it is not known whether any long-term gains were made by these subjects, it does seem likely that the abilities tested would relate to everyday listening situations where attention is interrupted and contextual cues, both before and after the interruption, are relied on heavily to 'fill the gaps'.

A study by Penfield and Marascuilo (1972) is interesting because of the differential effects of training in eleven comprehensive language listening skills. These skills ranged from 'inferring connotative meaning' up to higher order skills such as 'identifying sequence ambiguities'. Subjects were treated to a series of twenty-two lesson training periods in listening and two review sessions on the eleven skills.

The authors found that, '. . . whereas no SES (Socio—Economic Status) differences were uncovered at grade 2, by the time pupils reached grade 5, there was a distinct change in performance favouring the students at the high SES level.'

It was discovered that training procedure was highly effective at grade 2, and although only moderately effective at grade 5, the training narrowed the gap between SES levels at both grades in terms of listening attainment.

Those results strongly suggest the effectiveness of aural training (in these skills at least) in diminishing the differentials between high SES and low SES levels, which on most other indicators appear to increase as each successive year is spent in school.

In order to substantiate more fully the findings of research such as that just described, it is necessary to know whether the areas of listening skills isolated do relate to meaningful language situations. As stated previously the validity of the measures used must be examined critically. It would also be necessary to have some indication of the permanence of any gains shown. Unfortunately, much is as yet unknown.

Working on somewhat different lines, Wilkinson and Stratta (1972) at

122

the Oracy Research Unit at Birmingham University, are attempting to apply a number of questions to aural communications, which may be applied to any form of communication. Thus this approach, if successful, could facilitate a high degree of positive transfer from one communication system to another. The emphasis in this work is on relating listening to the interest and knowledge of the listener.

These researchers are justifiably critical of the kinds of material used in listening training, much of which is merely printed communication spoken aloud. It would seem pertinent to note at this point that passages which have been equated in terms of reading difficulty are not necessarily equal in terms of listening difficulty, as a study of Enc and Stolurow (1960) has shown. However, an experimental investigation by the writer has confirmed that two reading test passages chosen for their equivalence in terms of Rogers's (1962) formula for equating listening difficulty, were in fact equivalent.

The importance of some nonlinguistic factors in training aural skills should not be forgotten. A study by Pratt (1956) found that the effect of 'set' on a listener could be marked. Variables such as comfort of sitting position, attention to speaker's face, and a willingness to think about the ideas expressed were all relevant.

While caution is advocated in interpreting listening tests, this should not be taken to imply that some specific skills included in tests (e.g. auditory sequencing and auditory discrimination) are not to be taught as valuable listening skills. Merely it is intended to emphasize that there is a danger of defining listening too narrowly. (The same difficulties arise with definitions of reading: see United Kingdom Reading Association's (1972) evidence to the Bullock Committee.) A musical analogy is that if one is too concerned with identifying all the musical instruments used in a symphony, and the sequence in which they are played, one runs the risk of being unable to appreciate the piece as a whole.

Listening skills in relation to improving reading skills

If one looks at the skills of comprehension in listening and in reading one is not surprised to find certain very similar, if not identical, skill elements. As Gates (1962) aptly puts it:

> Comprehension in reading should be as intelligent, as subtle, as selective, as varied in character during reading as during listening. It is well to keep this in mind when considering the question of the variety of ways in which children can comprehend in reading. Actually, except as mechanical factors interfere, a child's intellectual activities in understanding, appreciating, and evaluating should be the same during reading as during listening.

Hollingsworth (1967) in a review of researches on the effect of listening in relation to reading concluded, 'Many of these research reports show that through improvement of listening abilities reading can be improved. Listening does have a positive effect on reading achievement.'

Bracken (1972) quoting the above statement, suggested that reading skills be taught through listening. However, the question remains as to which reading skills can be effectively taught through listening procedures. Whether improvement in any listening skill brings about an improvement in reading is still open to question.

When Kennedy (1971) trained one experimental group of underachieving readers in cloze-type listening skills he found that they did better on a cloze-type listening post-test but no better on a cloze-type reading post-test. The improvement of this listening skill brought about no improvement in the related reading skill.

Kelty (1953) and Lewis (1951), quoted by Bracken (1972) found that particular higher order skills such as understanding the main idea of the passage, drawing a conclusion, and predicting outcomes could be trained in listening and produce a significant degree of positive transfer to reading; such effects are compatible with the analysis of comprehension in reading and listening given by Gates (1962) earlier.

Teachers should be wary of drawing the conclusion that because a particular listening skill has been taught there will be a corresponding improvement in reading skills. There may well be good reason for teaching certain listening skills in their own right, but before claiming that practice in listening skills will improve reading skills, a careful analysis of the particular skills involved is essential.

Aural methodology and materials
The following is a brief outline of some aural methods and materials, both commercial and home-made, which appear relevant to the development of reading skills and listening skills.

Reading materials

Ricoh Synchrofax (E. J. Arnold, Leeds)
This apparatus is popularly known as the 'audio page' since the recorded message and the written message are each contained on either side of a work card which is fitted onto a playback/record machine. Although not much material has been produced commercially for this machine, blank pages are available cheaply for teachers to prepare their own audio work cards.

Language master (Bell and Howell)
This popular machine also combines the aural and visual message on cards which are fed through a playback machine. It is probably quite useful for building up a basal sight vocabulary and for learning short phrases, as well as for various phonic word sorting games. One major disadvantage is that long sentences or paragraphs cannot be fed into it. There is also no way of guaranteeing that the relevant part of the visual display is being attended to simultaneously with the aural display.

Remedial supply company tapes and materials
Although the booklets supplied with the reel tapes in this series are some-what old fashioned in flavour, it is one of the more comprehensive aural approaches to reading. Prereading aural discrimination exercises and repetition of vocabulary, adequate for all but the slowest learner, are two of the features which recommend this series for remedial groups.

Auditory discrimination exercises
A necessary first step in the development of phonic skills is that the learner recognizes regularities in spoken English words. Adequate aural discrimination skills are needed to note these regularities. Evans (1970) reported on a number of experiments which showed that normal auditory discrimination tests gave little indication of which children needed practice in these skills.

It is suggested that before verbal discrimination is attempted, attention is turned to discriminating familiar nonverbal sounds. Once the child has experience with attending to nonverbal sounds, discrimination exercises of the verbal type are introduced. In these one word is followed by another after a short pause, and the child is required to record whether the words are the same or different.

Yet another exercise is the recorded repetition of consonants or vowel digraphs with some examples following and the child is required to underline all the words on a prepared worksheet which either begin with, include, or end with these letters.

An exercise in which the child is required to order a number of cards showing certain unambiguous sound symbols in the order which is presented aurally can also be used.

These activities need to be carefully graded in the first stages and care must be taken in not presenting similar sounds contiguously.

Auditory sequencing exercises
Children needing practice in this skill can be diagnosed by an inability to recall short sequences of numbers or letters. Again, the progression from the familiar nonverbal to the verbal is suggested. A carefully graded series of prerecorded commands such as 'Put the green hat on the blue doll' leads to more complex tasks such as 'Write the numbers 3, 6, 1, 8, 2, 3' or 'Write the second letter in this series: B, C, X, Q, U, A.'

It is, of course, necessary to ascertain that the elements included in these commands (numbers, colours, letters, etc) are known before presentation.

Listening and Reading (British Broadcasting Corporation and Penguin Education)
The BBC has broadcast a series of radio programmes, meant for taping, designed for listening whilst following the text. The texts follow the broadcasts word for word and the three series so far produced cater for children aged six plus to eleven plus. Penguin have now published the booklets and cassettes for the stories in series one and two. All the stories are also included on a double LP from Penguin. The BBC publishes the booklets

quite inexpensively without the colourful illustrations included in the Penguin books. This is a most promising series.

Taped stories

Children's readers can be recorded and via headphones small groups allowed to follow the text. Some means can be utilized to ensure that attention is paid to the text such as bleeps obliterating the occasional word and requiring the child to write down the word which is missed out. Words can be added or left out and the child can be required to spot the 'mistakes' or merely to count the number of 'mistakes' made.

'Take Part' play readings (Penguin Education)

This fast-expanding series of play reading books caters for mixed-ability groups reading aloud to each other. Each play reading part is of a certain level of reading difficulty from about six years reading age to nine plus years reading age. Some of the simpler parts amount to little more than repeating a phrase previously spoken or inserting an animal noise, but poorer readers certainly get a boost from being able to join in and also profit in following the text while more able readers read their parts aloud. The publishers suggest that the plays are recorded and that the children be allowed to insert their own sound effects. Appropriate points for sound effects are marked with an asterisk on the text.

A possibility for compressed tapes

Looking to the future it may be possible, if facilities for compressing tapes become readily available, to have the same material recorded at different rates of compression (or expansion) and to use them as pacers for developing fluency. Neville and Pugh (1973) have reported some success in using such methods with students learning English as a second language.

Listening materials

Listening Skill Builders (Science Research Associates)

A series of exercises included in some of the SRA *Reading Laboratories* are claimed to be of use in developing listening skills. A story is read to the children and then they are required to answer a number of multiple choice questions based on the text and also to put in the correct order a number of (supposedly) relevant details from the text. The writer has found the material itself to be most unimaginative in style and content, and that many alternatives to the correct responses in the multiple choice items are not viable answers to the questions asked. Moreover, the material is literal rather than aural and many of the questions are somewhat trivial.

Listening Laboratory Ib (Science Research Associates)

Having, no doubt, become aware of some of the limitations of the Listening Skill Builders, SRA has produced a laboratory (the first in a series) specifically designed to develop particular listening skills for seven to eight year olds. Some of the skills isolated for training would appear to be appropriate in developing parallel reading skills. Twenty-eight professionally produced listening passages (complete with music and sound effects) are used to develop seven component listening comprehension skills.

Listening with understanding (A unit of the Concept 7-9 materials produced by the Schools Council and published by E. J. Arnold)
These materials, developed by the Schools Council, are designed for the infant/junior transition period and consist of a number of cassettes (or Arnold's 'packettes') with recorded graded exercises in a number of elementary listening skills. The lessons are short, and somewhat complex linguistically, requiring careful attention and often repetition. Though not very stimulating material, profitable use could be made of it to supplement a fuller and more creative approach to developing listening skills.

Language Centre 2 (Drake Educational Associates, Cardiff)
One section of these multilevel language arts materials (the first in a series) deals with developing listening skills in the seven to eight age group. Four component listening skills are isolated and tested by multiple choice questions after the listening passage.

Conclusion
Not all children will profit from practice in all the exercises and materials outlined above. It is important that some informal diagnosis be undertaken instead of adopting the materials and exercises wholesale. It should be remembered that although improvement in some listening skills undoubtedly improves some reading skills, there are areas of reading and listening which are probably not closely related and yet worthy of individual attention in a language arts curriculum.

References
BEKESY, G. VON (1957) *The Ear* Scientific American reprint: W. H. Freeman and Company
BEVER, T. (1968) *Communication by Language: The Reading Process* Proceedings of Conference of National Institute of Child Health and Human Development, New Orleans, February
BRACKEN, D. K. (1972) 'Research and practice in improving listening' in V. Southgate (Ed) *Literacy at All Levels* London: Ward Lock Educational
DEVINE, T. G. (1967) Listening *Review of Educational Research* 37, 152-8
ELLIS, H. (1965) *The Transfer of Learning* New York: Macmillan
ENC, M. E. and STOLUROW, L. M. (1960) A comparison of the effects of two recording speeds on learning and retention *New Outlook for the Blind* 54, 39-48
EVANS, A. J. (1970) 'Promoting reading readiness: methods and materials' in M. Chazan (Ed) *Reading Readiness* Swansea: University College of Swansea Faculty of Education

FOULKE, E. (1968) *Communication by Language: The Reading Process* Proceedings of Conference of National Institute of Child Health and Human Development New Orleans, February

FOULKE, E. and STICHT, T. G. (1969) A review of research on the intelligibility and comprehension of accelerated speech *Psychological Bulletin* 72, 1, 50-62

GATES, A. I. (1962) *The Improvement of Reading* New York: Macmillan

HOLLINGSWORTH, P. M. (1967) 'Can training in listening improve reading?' in W. K. Durr (Ed) *Reading Instruction Dimensions and Issues* Boston: Houghton Mifflin

HOLT, J. (1967) *How Children Learn* Harmondsworth: Penguin

KELTY, A. (1953) *An experimental study to determine the effects of listening for certain purposes upon achievement of reading for those purposes* Unpublished doctoral dissertation, Colorado State College of Education

KENNEDY, D. K. and WEENER, J. (1973) *Training in the cloze procedure, visually and auditorially, to improve the reading and listening comprehension of third grade underachieving readers* Doctoral dissertation: Pennsylvania State University

LEWIS, M. S. (1951) *The effect of training in listening for certain purposes upon reading for those same purposes* Unpublished doctoral dissertation: Colorado State College of Education

MARTIN, C. (1955) Developmental interrelationships among language variables in children of first grade *Elementary English* 3, 2, 167-71

NEVILLE, N. H. and PUGH, A. K. (1973) An exploratory study of the application of time-compressed and time-expanded speech in the development of the English reading proficiency of foreign students *English Language Teaching* (in press)

PENFIELD, D. A. and MARASCUILO, L. A. (1972) Learning to listen: an experimental study *Educational Research* 14, 220-4

PRATT, E. (1956) Experimental evaluation of a program for the improvement of listening *Elementary School Journal* 56, 315-320

ROGERS, J. R. (1962) A formula for predicting the comprehension level of material to be presented orally *Journal of Educational Research* 56, 218-220

SOUTHGATE, V. (1970) 'The importance of structure in beginning reading' in K. Gardner (Ed) *Reading Skills: Theory and Practice* London: Ward Lock Educational

SPEARRITT, D. (1962) *Listening Comprehension: A Factorial Analysis* Australian Council for Education Research, Series No. 76 Melbourne: ACER

STEEN, A. M. (1969) *The effectiveness of listening lessons in the kindergarten as determined by the listening response test* Unpublished doctoral dissertation: University of Iowa

UNITED KINGDOM READING ASSOCIATION (1972) *Evidence presented to the committee of enquiry into reading and the use of English in schools* United Kingdom Reading Association, December

WILKINSON, A. and STRATTA, L. (1970) Listening comprehension at
13+ *Educational Review* 22, 228-42
WILKINSON, A. and STRATTA, L. (1972) Listening and the study of
spoken language *Educational Review* 25, 3-20

E

16 Factors affecting the efficient reading of science textbooks – a pilot study

H. C. Gillard

Introduction
The 'average' secondary school pupil is one who may expect to achieve a grade 4 pass at CSE. Such a pupil enjoys the practical aspects of science but finds textbook study arduous. Few secondary modern schools are able to allot enough time to science (often less than 65 per cent of that recommended by examiners). Textbook study is therefore essential for full syllabus coverage and must be carried out in the pupils' own time without teacher supervision or assistance.

The investigations described in this paper were made in an attempt to isolate and assess areas of difficulty so that practical guidance might be given to help pupils overcome them.

Groups studied
Two groups of children were studied in September 1972:

Group A	All first year pupils other than those in remedial classes. They were from seven primary schools and had no previous experience of formal science lessons.
Final sample	Ninety boys and girls: results showed no apparent sex differences.

Group B	All fourth year pupils entered for a science examination course. All had received three years of combined science lessons (physics, chemistry and biology).
Final sample	Thirty-three boys and twenty-three girls.

Presentation of results
The arbitrary nature of the groups finally selected and the empirical design of the tests make rigorous statistical analysis irrelevant. Test results are shown as line graphs using a common scale so that visual comparison is easy and trends may be clearly seen. Where appropriate the results are plotted in order of increasing VRQ (Murray House) or RQ (GAP Reading Test–Combined Scores). Both quotients are of known reliability and so provide useful parameters.

130

Graph 1 First year pupils RQ–VRQ

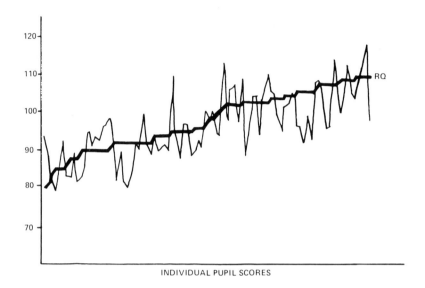

INDIVIDUAL PUPIL SCORES

Graph 2 First year–RQ/all science texts (cloze %)

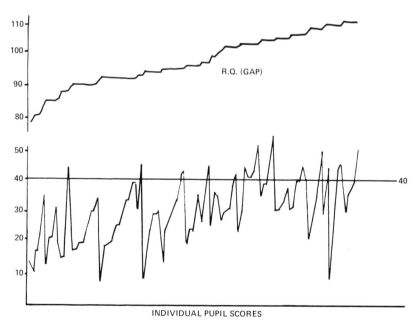

INDIVIDUAL PUPIL SCORES

Group A – Results

VRQ against RQ
Graph 1 shows the VRQ plotted in order of RQ. Despite wide individual variation in individual scores there is a clear rise of RQ with VRQ. Graph 1 shows a fortunate distribution—half the sample lies either side of RQ 100.

Cloze scores for science texts (tenth word deletions)
Graph 2 shows the mean of all three percentile scores in RQ order for physics, chemistry and biology. Below RQ 100 scores rise with RQ. Above RQ 100 and especially above RA 12.6, there is no further rise.

Bormuth (1968) proposes that cloze scores below 40 per cent identified materials too difficult for the pupils tested. On such a scale *all* the science texts used were too hard (see later discussion of textbook provision). An order of difficulty shows clearly, both by comparison of the whole score graphs and from the number of pupils scoring below 40 per cent for each subject. Physics is least difficult with forty-three pupils failing, chemistry next with seventy and biology worst with eighty-two. The mean score for all three subjects gave seventy-one pupils (80 per cent) failing to achieve 40 per cent.

It should be noted that, for all texts tested, some difficulty was experienced in finding representative passages of prose 200 to 250 words long. The situation revealed by the cloze tests is thus biased in favour of the texts which are even more complex than appears from this one measure.

Unknown word scores
Pupils were asked to read three typical pages of each textbook. They were required to list all words unknown to them. Scores were plotted in the same order as cloze test results.

Biology and physics scores were close and uniform. Chemistry scores were far more erratic and appear to have no relationship with cloze results. Again, a clear order of difficulty was apparent but this time biology was easiest (two pupils claiming more than twenty 'unknowns'), physics second, (five pupils claimed over twenty 'unknowns') and chemistry was clearly the worst with twenty pupils claiming more than twenty 'unknowns'— nine pupils over thirty!

Some bias in favour of biology may have occurred because many pupils came from primary schools with keen natural history clubs.

The general trend of scores is of particular interest. The 'unknown' line was virtually horizontal whilst the cloze line rose steadily for each text. Clearly, although vocabulary is important, it is a decreasing factor as comprehension skills increase. It would seem advisable, therefore, to give routine attention to vocabulary improvement by means of word lists and simple subject dictionaries. More powerful teaching effort may be better used in other areas.

Cloze scores for English textbooks, O level and CSE
The results showed a very close link between VRQ and cloze scores for CSE for *all* pupils with reading ages above 12.6 (the upper limit measured by the GAP test). Below 12.6 performances were erratic. There was no measurable difference between scores of boys and girls.

The O level text scores were very erratic, the only discernible trends being a slightly lower performance by the boys and a marked levelling off in the higher VRQ range. Clearly the level of comprehension expected of an O level candidate is much higher than that for CSE. Although such a distinction is to be expected, the erratic form of the plotted results would suggest that many factors were at work—an area needing close scrutiny because it is generally assumed that an O level science pupil is also at ease with O level English.

Cloze scores for science textbooks, O level and CSE
Four textbooks are in use—two for physics (one classed as CSE the other as dual CSE/O level), one dual role (CSE/O level) for each of chemistry and biology. Pupils were tested on all four books and subject scores expressed as percentiles.

Both sets of results clearly repeated the erratic form of the O level English scores—the results for the girls being more compact and some 8 per cent lower than the boys. Applying the 40 per cent rule, less than one third of the girls can cope with the texts (seven for biology, six for physics and three for chemistry). The boys are similarly weak in biology (seven) and chemistry (eight) with only one third able to cope but their physics competence is higher—half the sample can cope (seventeen).

With no sex difference for CSE English and a marginally lower boys performance at O level English there must be several factors unique to science to cause the wide contrast in boy/girl performances in physics. The present results would seem to confirm the long held belief that physics is 'a boys' subject'; they do *not*, however, support the equally long held view that all 'science' is for boys alone. By a fortunate chance subject-teacher variables may be excluded from these results because all the pupils tested had received the same course of physics (by a physics teacher), chemistry (by a chemistry teacher) and biology (by a biology teacher). Is there perhaps a national sex/science ability correlation?

Motivation may play a major part in the scores (see later notes on pupils' reasons for taking a science). Unlike the first year scores there is no discernible rank order for the separate disciplines, despite long standing evidence (from the school records) that pupils are biased either to physics and physics/chemistry or to biology and biology/chemistry. There is only one case of a pupil taking physics and biology in the last eight years.

Despite these apparent confusions two major trends are clear:

1   There is no increase of science reading skill with rising VRQ.

2   There is no increase of science reading skill with rising English reading skill.

Science reading skills must therefore be taught.

Factors determining textbooks used

In the primary school, and in the English lessons of the lower years of the secondary school, textbooks are chosen to match pupils' reading skills. The books are, in effect, matched to the pupils. In science classes at the secondary stage no such matching occurs.

In an attempt to quantify the factors which affect textbook choice, a number of Hampshire schools were sent a questionnaire concerning science texts and related matters. Completion of the questionnaire was voluntary and care was taken to ensure that teachers and schools concerned would be anonymous. To avoid possible bias the authors' school was not included. Five schools returned the questionnaire. Four reported complete freedom of choice, by staff, of textbooks used; one did not refer to that aspect.

Schools were asked to rate eleven possible factors in order of importance and to indicate to what factor, if any, they were forced to give priority. Results are given in Table 1 below.

Table 1

Factor	School order					Nett order
	A	B	C	D	E	
Date of publication	3	6	2	7	2	5
Reputation of author	11	5	2	7	3	6
Largest coverage of syllabus	7	1	1	1	1	1
Practical work content	5	2	1	4	7	4
Descriptions of experiments	6	2	1	5	6	5
Academic standard of text	4	2	1	7	5	4
Cost per book	2	3	1	7	4	3
Simplicity of language	1	3	1	2	9	2
Provision of test questions	10	4	1	6	8	7
Number of photos	8	2	1	7	10	6
Number of line diagrams	9	4	1	3	11	6

Three schools said they were forced to give cost priority, the other two were 'free' but one of them rated cost third in order of priority. Simplicity of language, though rated a nett second, is closely followed by academic standard (fourth), so that the pupil must finally be faced with a text chosen with almost no concern for his individual reading skills.

The situation of the pupil may be seen to be worsened by the following summary of the replies, by eighteen teachers, to other questions:

1   Eleven had heard of readability.
2   Readability 'had significance' for nine.
3   Five (all in one school) knew the Reading Ages of their exam pupils.
4   Two had heard of cloze procedure and one of them had carried out a cloze test on a science text.
5   Ten rated their pupils' reading skills as 'adequate', eight rated them 'poor'. Two teachers in the one school differed between 'adequate' and 'poor' for the same pupils!

In all the schools exam pupils had their own textbooks and were allowed to take them home. First year pupils were sometimes allowed to take books home, the majority had to share books in class.

Why pupils choose science
Three schools allowed pupils to answer, anonymously, the following questions for which replies have been totalled:

'Are you taking this exam because'	Physics	Chemistry	Biology
1 You like it?	26	32	127
2 You chose it rather than do the others?			28
3 You need it for your future job?	39		6
4 It's another exam to get?	4	4	5

There are clear signs that pupil motivation varies widely within and between subjects.

Reading subskills
Bond and Wagner (1966), in addition to basic comprehension, identify seventeen groups of 'basic study skills' needed for successful reading. Herber (1970) in a survey of opinions of teachers, authors of reading texts, and reading journals, lists no less than ninety-nine separate 'factors' which may occur in different reading 'areas'. Herber also makes a neat distinction between 'transfer'—the application of early reading skills to later work—and 'transformation', which he defines as 'the adaptation of a skill or process to meet the demands of material peculiar to a content area'. By such semantic arguments he maintains that there are *no* separate subject reading skills. This may be true at university levels of scholarships but is not so for the average pupil with whom this paper is concerned.

The average pupil sees 'maths' as 'maths' not as 'part of science'; he sees 'English' as 'English' not as 'part of history or science'. It is as if each subject is kept in a mental box of its own. The child is not sufficiently mentally mature to see the general utility of his knowledge.

Clearly the reading skills of science must be taught as separate items, not merely adapted from other disciplines.

Textbook profiles

In order to determine the subskills necessary to the successful use of science texts, a method of textbook assessment has been developed which identifies separate skills and roughly determines their relative importance in any one text. The method has been used by teachers and older pupils for both science and geography. It results in a histogram and can be applied to examination papers as well as textbooks.

Method

1 Count the number of pages of text, excluding index, contents, preface and introduction.
2 On scrap paper list columns headed for the various items likely to be met.
3 Go through the book scoring a mark under each column for every page on which the item appears. Do not score each occurrence—merely each page on which an item occurs.
4 Total the marks for each column and express them as a percentage of the number of pages.
5 Draw a simple histogram of the results for future reference.

In many cases stage 3 is quite sufficient since the marks themselves form a rough profile.

It has been found to take less than an hour to complete all five stages for a large science or geography text. The examples shown here indicate the contrast of skills between subjects and the varying emphasis placed upon them by examiners and authors.

Publishers could issue profiles for textbooks without any appreciable increase in production cost. A study of a textbook profile will lead to a more objective assessment of its complexity than is usually made. If a cloze test were to be included as suggested by Gilliland (1972), the stage would be set for a positive effort at developing appropriate reading skills.

Examination of the science profiles shows the need for detailed teaching of diagrams, drawings, tables and graphs as well as the traditional topics of symbols and equations. The predominance of the illustrative items may well increase the problem of comprehension because many science texts are concise and assume an understanding of illustrated concepts which are not explained in words.

Teaching methods—research

In Britain there is virtually no research into secondary school science reading skills. There are a few recent references to the need to teach science reading skills and many complaints about the lack of such skills beyond the primary stage. Several commercial courses and texts exist for 'efficient reading', all of which deal with *speed*. The object of such courses is to permit a rapid impression to be formed of narrative, technical prose rather than complex, condensed study data. Based on American research into eye movement drills such courses are very effective, but have no value for secondary school work.

Table 2 First year science textbook profiles

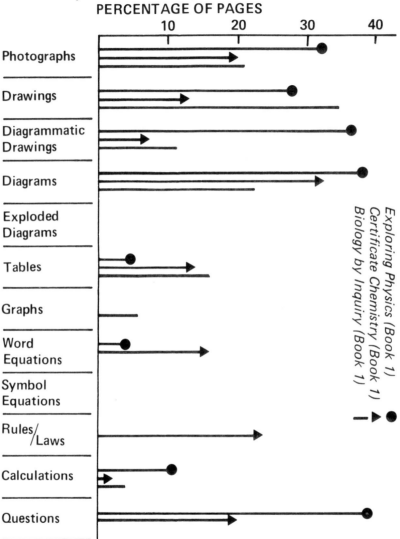

Despite the wealth of American research on reading, there is very little which refers directly to science. One or two minor papers refer to possible correlations between science skill and history or mathematics. Other papers, in the educational technology field, consider the effects of colour versus black and white in photos and illustrations—to no definite end. Two major texts do have worthwhile material although both refer to science texts which we would use with junior or remedial classes.

Bond and Wagner (1966) devote some ten pages to discussion illustrating their ideas with a fifth grade (eleven plus) text of a very simple kind.

137

Their excellent bibliography of 285 items lists only seven which have any relevance for science. Summarized, they refer to problems of vocabulary and technical comprehension and suggest a practical approach using the texts as a form of work card.

Herber (1970) is more detailed. He lists twenty-five science references from a total of 226 and gives some reading exercises based on a ninth grade (fifteen plus) text of very general use which corresponds roughly to a second/third year basic text for our secondary pupils. His list of factors referred to earlier is of considerable value as are his systems for developing comprehension at varying levels.

Current small-scale work into programmed booklets for teaching vocabulary is being carried out by Townsend together with directed reading programmes and linear programmes for using graphs and photos by Gillard. Results are not expected before late 1974.

Summary

The average pupil needs direct teaching in order to make proper use of science textbooks. By the end of the third year of secondary schooling some sex and subject differences appear. Vocabulary is important but *not* the dominant factor. Comprehension exercises are needed for prose but must be supported by detailed instruction in the use and interpretation of graphs, tables, symbols, etc. Much measured study is needed in these areas.

References

BOND, G. L. and WAGNER, E. B. (1966) *Teaching the Child to Read* New York: Macmillan

BORMUTH, J. R. (1968) Cloze test readability: criterion reference scores *Journal of Educational Measurement* 5, 189-96

GILLILAND, J. (1972) *Readability* UKRA Teaching of Reading Monograph London: University of London Press

HERBER, H. L. (1970) *Teaching Reading in Content Areas* New Jersey: Prentice Hall

17 The development of reading, writing and other communication skills during the comprehensive and upper secondary school years: presentation of a Swedish research project

Hans Grundin

Functional literacy: a major goal of reading instruction

A major objective of modern school education is to develop the students' skills so as to make them as capable as possible of independent study. The Swedish comprehensive school curriculum (Skolöverstyrelsen 1969) gives the following guidelines for the orientation subjects, '. . . it is important to teach the students where information can be acquired, to train them to select broad and diverse materials and evaluate them independently, to teach them study techniques and form good study habits, and to try to stimulate their interest in independent study.' Communication skills, especially reading, are obviously of vital importance, if such goals are to be attained.

Reading and other communication skills are, however, more than study tools. They are necessary instruments for the development of men and women as individuals and citizens. This has been emphasized by Malmquist (1969), who also points out that literacy in a traditional sense is not enough, that we must 'raise our sights about functional literacy' since 'in many highly industrialized countries workers will by 1980 need a reading capacity of even a twelfth-grade level'.

If we accept high level 'functional literacy' as the long-term goal of instruction in reading and other communication skills, it is quite clear that the development of these skills must continue throughout the school. The need for continued reading training at the higher school levels does not seem generally realized in Swedish schools. The situation seems similar in most countries in Europe, since the development of reading skills at higher school levels has been the object of very few studies (Malmquist 1970). In England, Gardner (1972) concluded from a study of some 1,400 technical college students aged from fifteen to twenty years that, 'the evidence seems to indicate that young people are rather ill-equipped to gain either information or pleasure from print'.

To sum up the present discussion it may be noted, then, that functional literacy at a high level is the long-term goal of instruction in reading and related communication skills, and that continued training throughout the secondary school is necessary in order to reach this goal.

Background of the present study

The development of reading and writing skills during the first school years has been the object of rather detailed study in Sweden in recent years. A number of studies in this field were conducted for Educational Research in Linköping by Eve Malmquist (see Malmquist 1969). The study of reading and other communication skills at other school levels has not reached a similar breadth, however. In view of their great importance and the fact that they cannot be regarded as fully developed during the primary school years the lack of studies of the development of such skills at the higher school levels has been felt as a serious deficiency.

It seemed, therefore, an important task for Swedish reading research to study the development of different communication skills from the school start at the age of seven to the end of the upper secondary school at the age of nineteen. This would make it possible to determine in what respects and at what ages an improved training of these skills is called for.

Purpose of the study

The main purposes of the project presented here are:

1 to describe the development from seven to nineteen years of certain reading, writing and other communication skills.
2 to investigate to what extent the objectives, concerning the skills studied, of current comprehensive and upper secondary school curricula can be regarded as reached at different age levels.

The skills studied are primarily such skills as practically all young persons need or can be expected to need, regardless of the occupations they choose when they leave school.

Construction and selection of tests

The research at the National School for Educational Research in Linköping referred to above resulted in, among other things, the construction and standardization of a series of reading and writing tests for the ages seven to ten years. Some of these were employed in the present project. For the other ages involved (eleven to nineteen years) it proved, however, necessary to construct some new tests, especially as regards more 'practical' reading and writing skills.

It was also necessary to assess the usefulness of different tests at age levels other than those for which they were originally constructed. Most standardized tests are intended for one particular school level only. When one wishes to describe the development of different skills during many grade levels, it is, however, desirable that each test be applicable to all, or at least several grade levels. In a study including students from twelve different grades it is, of course, not possible to employ the same test battery for all groups. It was therefore decided to use different test batteries at different levels with a certain 'overlap' between the batteries, i.e. some groups are given both the easy and the intermediate variants of a test, or both the intermediate and the difficult variants. This overlapping is illustrated in Table 1, where the whole set of tests employed in the project is presented.

Table 1 Overview of the tests used within the project and the grade levels at which they have been given

Test	1	2	3	4	5	6	7	8	9	10	11	12
LF 1: Reading comprehension	▬	▬	▬									
LF 2: Reading comprehension		▬	▬									
LF 3: Reading comprehension					▬	▬	▬	▬	▬			
LH 1: Reading rate	▬	▬	▬									
LH 2: Reading rate					▬	▬	▬	▬	▬	▬	▬	▬
RS 1: Spelling	▬	▬	▬									
RS 2: Spelling			▬	▬	▬	▬	▬	▬	▬	▬	▬	▬
RS 3: Spelling			▬	▬	▬	▬	▬	▬	▬			
AS: Transcription				▬	▬	▬	▬	▬	▬	▬	▬	▬
A: Alphabet				▬	▬	▬	▬	▬	▬	▬	▬	▬
PS: Creative writing				▬	▬	▬	▬	▬	▬	▬	▬	▬
LT: Cloze test			▬	▬	▬	▬	▬	▬	▬	▬	▬	▬
PRL 1: 'Practical' reading						▬	▬	▬	▬	▬	▬	▬
PRL 2: 'Practical' reading						▬	▬	▬	▬	▬	▬	▬
PRS: 'Practical' reading and writing							▬	▬	▬	▬	▬	▬

Note: The comprehensive school (*grundskola*) comprises grades 1-9 with three levels including three grades each. Grades 10-12 constitute the Swedish *gymnasieskola,* in which some sections consist of grades 10-11 only.

By means of the overlapping explained above it should be possible to 'translate' actual results in one test to estimated results in another, e.g. results in tests LF 2 for grades three and four could be 'translated' to estimated results in test LF 3, which was not given in any grade below grade five.

Three tests were given in all twelve grades, namely AS, a transcription test, A, an alphabet test, and PS, a free writing test. One test was given in all grades but the first, namely LT, a cloze test. Starting with grade six of the comprehensive school, one and the same test battery, containing ten tests, was employed in all grades. Thus, the design permits direct comparisons between students of different grade levels over an interval of at least seven grades—and in some cases twelve grades. Apart from the possibilities provided by the overlapping design (see above) the data will permit direct comparisons between widely different age groups as to their skills in different respects—something which is rather unique in the study of reading and related communication skills.

Brief descriptions of the tests

The reading comprehension tests (LF 1-3 in Table 1) are of a rather conventional type with paragraphs of continuous prose text followed by one or more multiple-choice questions. Each test contains about fifteen items and the testing time varies from four minutes (LF 1) to twelve minutes (LF 2 and 3).

The reading rate tests (LH 1-2) both consist of a continuous prose text where a word has been deleted on every fifth or so line and replaced by a parenthesis containing three alternative words. The subject has to underline the word which fits into the text. The test items are easy, so that almost any student who has read the text with some care can select the right word instantaneously. Therefore, the tests can be considered as primarily tests of reading rate and only secondarily as tests of reading comprehension. The testing time is six minutes for each test.

The spelling tests (RS 1-3) are of the dictation type, i.e. the tester reads a sentence, e.g. 'Bo has fine teeth', and then instructs the students to write a word in that sentence, 'Write *teeth*!' Each test contains fifteen items. In all grades where two RS tests were given, i.e. grades three to twelve, the two tests were administered in a sequence so that they appeared as one test to the students.

In the transcription test (AS) the students were instructed to copy fast but also correctly a printed prose text. They were allowed to use any kind of handwriting. They were also informed that the test was not a test of calligraphy, but that any legible handwriting would be accepted. The testing time was six minutes.

In the test A the students are simply instructed to write the Swedish alphabet with the letters in correct order, starting with 'a'.

The cloze test (LT) is a slightly modified version of a test constructed in accordance with the procedure defined by Taylor (1953). It consists of a continuous prose text of 210 words with every fifth word deleted and replaced by a space of uniform length. The modification consisted of re-writing parts of the original text in order to avoid some ambiguous items. In the correction of this test the replies, i.e. the words filled in by the students, are evaluated not only as to their agreement with the original text, as in the mechanical correction of cloze tests (cf. Bormuth 1968), but also as to their semantic and grammatical correctness. A test of this type can be regarded as primarily a reading comprehension test, and usually correlates highly with conventional comprehension tests (cf. e.g. Bormuth 1968 and 1969). The testing time was ten minutes for this test.

In the creative writing test (PS) the students were given twenty minutes to write a brief essay on possible means to improve road traffic safety. This topic was chosen because it was thought that students of all ages would have both some personal experiences and some educational experience to draw upon, since traffic education starts already in grade one in Swedish schools. The analysis of the essays will be restricted to certain quantitative aspects of the students' productivity and of the language employed in their writing such as number of words written, mean clause length (in the sense of Hunt 1966) and proportion of 'long' words as a measure of how advanced their vocabulary is (cf. Bjornsson 1968, Bormuth 1966).

The 'practical' reading and writing tests (PRL 1-2, PRS), finally, contain selected tasks which any young adult may meet in his or her personal or occupational life. PRL 1 is a reading comprehension test that requires very close and careful reading: it contains authentic insurance policy terms and eight test items in which the student is to decide whether the insurance covers certain damages wholly, partly or not at all. PRL 2 contains tables and instructions from which the housing allowances for families of different types and with different incomes can be determined. The students are given three test items asking them to determine the amount of housing allowance under different circumstances. PRS contains three authentic forms, which the students are asked to fill in according to instructions given in the test. Two of them are postal forms and the third is a form which every Swedish citizen has to fill in when reporting his income to the general health insurance authority.

Student sample and testing procedure

The student sample comprises about 210 students from each of the twelve grades concerned, making a total of more than 2,500 students. About ten entire classes were sampled for each grade level, including both normal classes and special classes (e.g. reading classes, school readiness classes and classes for the mentally retarded). The sampling was confined to the municipality of Linköping (population about 110,000).

The tests were administered by testers, engaged and trained for this purpose, at the end of the spring term 1972. In order to make possible an assessment of the increase in the skills studied at different grade levels, the same test batteries were administered once again one year later, in May or June 1973. This procedure may of course entail some undesirable 'test learning' effects, which will be added to the 'true' increase in the students' skills. Since the students—and their teachers—had no possibilities of studying the tests between the two test occasions, we believe, however, that this effect is quite small.

The marking of the tests and the registration of test data are performed in such a way as to permit analyses at the level of the individual test items. It will thus be possible to determine, for each test item, the grade level at which the item is mastered by a given proportion of the students.

Some observations made during the testing periods

The variability in performance was large at all grade levels, not only between individuals but also between classes within the same grade level. There seems to be reason to believe that this is due not only to differences between classes as to the ability of the students and the competence of the teachers but also to motivational factors. In some classes the students seemed very eager to do their best, while in other classes many students seemed to care much less about their test performance.

The motivation of the students in the test situation also appears to vary with the grade or age level, i.e. it is at a constant high level—or even increasing—through grades one to six and then decreases in the higher grades. The extent of this decrease seems to depend on some 'classroom climate' factors though, since it is very noticeable in certain classes and hardly observable at all in others.

On the whole, most students made serious attempts to solve the tasks. It was quite clear, though, that the tests which kept the students more or less constantly busy reading, copying a text or checking given response alternatives were preferred to tests demanding a more creative effort. The test causing the most negative reactions was the PS test, where the students were supposed to compose a short essay in twenty minutes. Many students —especially in the higher grades—claimed the testing time was *too long*. This may again be a question of motivation, and the students might have found another topic for this essay test more inspiring. Nevertheless, the negative reactions to the testing time—and not to the task—in the PS test were so common that it must be assumed that many of the students in this study are not very accustomed to essay writing.

Some preliminary results

The analysis of the vast amount of data collected in this study (corresponding to more than 300 punch card columns for each of more than 2,500 subjects) is still under way. Some preliminary data are, however, already available. A few samples of these will be given below.

Reading comprehension in grades five to twelve as measured by the test LF3 (see page 141) is illustrated in Figure 1. The figure gives, for each grade, the tenth, thirtieth, fiftieth, seventieth and ninetieth percentiles, expressed as proportions (in per cent) of the maximum score for the test. Figure 1 shows clearly that reading comprehension is increasing continuously from grade five to grade eleven. The rate of increase is approximately the same at all levels of ability (the percentile curves are roughly parallel). Still, the overlapping between grades is considerable. The poorest readers in grade twelve (below P_{10}) score, for instance, below the median (P_{50}) of grade five, and the best readers in grades five and six equal the average readers in grade eleven or grade twelve.

It is noticeable that the curve connecting median values (P_{50}) for the different grades is quite smooth, even in the transition from the end of the compulsory comprehensive school (grade nine) to the upper secondary school (grades ten to twelve). This probably reflects the fact that the upper secondary school in Sweden (*gymnasieskolan*) is not very selective, since it recruits in many communities more than 80 per cent of the seventeen year olds. With a highly selective upper secondary school one would, of course, have expected a much more marked difference between grade nine and grade ten than between grades eight and nine or grades ten and eleven.

Figure 1 Preliminary summary of reading comprehension test (LF 3) results for grades 5-12. (P_{10}=10th percentile)

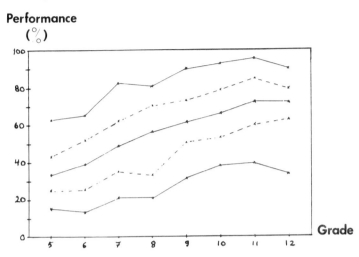

Performance (%)

Grade

Results for grades six to twelve on the PRS test, which may be called a 'form comprehension test' (see page 146) are summarized in Figure 2, which is analogous to Figure 1. Here again there is a marked increase in test scores from grade six to grade eleven at all percentile levels. The variability tends to decrease with increasing grade level, but this may partly be due to a so-called ceiling effect in grades ten to twelve. The overlap between grades is still considerable, but less marked than in the case of reading comprehension (cf. Figure 1). The tenth percentile for grades eleven and twelve, for instance, is above the seventieth percentile for grade six. The data reported here seem to indicate that the ability to comprehend and fill in forms increases more rapidly during grades seven to eleven than does general reading comprehension. This may be due to the fact that 'form filling' skills are normally not systematically trained before grade seven in the Swedish comprehensive school, whereas general reading comprehension skills are, of course, trained from the very beginning of the comprehensive school.

Spelling ability in grades five to twelve was measured by the test RS3. A preliminary summary of test results is shown in Figure 3, which is analogous to Figures 1 and 2 above. As in the previous figures we find a steady increase in test score up to grade eleven for all percentile levels—except, perhaps, for the ninetieth percentile, where ceiling effects occur in the higher grades. It is noteworthy that this increase in spelling performance from grade to grade is about as rapid for poor spellers (P_{10}) as for average spellers (P_{50}). There is a great deal of overlap between grades, but it is noteworthy that the tenth percentile for grade twelve is well above the seventieth percentile

145

Figure 2 Preliminary summary of 'form comprehension' test (PRS) results for grades 6-12. (P$_{10}$=10th percentile etc.)

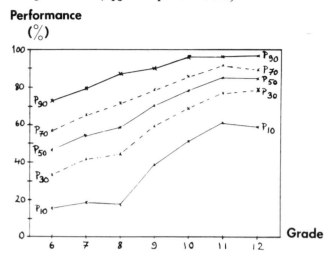

Figure 2 Preliminary summary of 'form comprehension' test (PRS) results for grades 6-12. (P$_{10}$=10th percentile etc.)

for grade six and equals the median for grade eight. As in the case of the other two tests (Figures 1 and 2) the transition from the comprehensive (grade nine) to the upper secondary school (grade ten) shows no sign of disruption of the smooth percentile curves. The spelling data reported cannot tell us whether spelling ability in the Swedish comprehensive or upper secondary school is good or bad, but they do tell that this ability is continuously increasing from grade to grade until the age of eighteen.

Figure 3 Preliminary summary of spelling test (RS 3) results for grades 5-12. (P$_{10}$=10th percentile etc.)

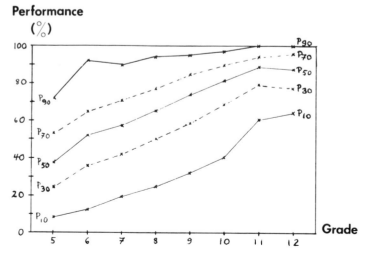

Much more could be said about the data presented here and similar figures could be provided for the other tests used in the project. This would, however, lead far beyond the scope of the present paper.

Completion of the project

The collection of test data was completed in June 1973 and the data analysis will take place in the academic year 1973/74. During the same period there will also be an analysis of the objectives of the Swedish comprehensive school (*grundskola*) and upper secondary school (*gymnasieskola*) as to the skills studies in this project. Since the written curricula provide little guidance for establishing the degrees of skill students are supposed to attain, a questionnaire procedure will be employed in order to establish the opinion of different 'interest groups' in this respect. The final project report will be forthcoming in 1974.

References

BJORNSSON, C. H. (1968) *Läsbarhet (Readability)* Stockholm: Liber

BORMUTH, J. R. (1966) Readability: a new approach *Reading Research Quarterly* 1, 79-132

BORMUTH, J. R. (1968) The cloze readability procedure *Elementary English* 45, 429-36

BORMUTH, J. R. (1969) Factor validity of cloze tests as measures of reading comprehension ability *Reading Research Quarterly* 4, 358-65

GARDNER, J. (1972) 'The student reader' in A. Melnik and J. Merritt (Eds) *Reading: Today and Tomorrow* London: University of London Press

HUNT, K. W. (1966) Recent measures in syntactic development *Elementary English* 43, 732-39

MALMQUIST, E. (1969) 'Reading: A human right and a human problem' in R. C. Staiger and O. Andresen (Eds) *Proceedings of the Second World Congress on Reading* Linköping: IRA

MALMQUIST, E. (1970) A decade of reading research in Europe 1959-1969: A review *The Journal of Educational Research* 63, 309-29

SKOLOVERSTYRELSEN (1969) *Läroplan för Grundskolan: Allmän del (Curriculum for the Comprehensive School: General Part)* Stockholm: Utbildningsförlaget

TAYLOR, W. L. (1953) Cloze procedure: a new tool for measuring readability *Journalism Quarterly* 30, 415-33

18 The reading habits and interests of adolescents and adults

E. J. Hayes

Adult reading

A most disturbing finding is that 60 per cent of young people become reading dropouts. The Crowther Report (1959), The International Publishing Corporation (1966) and Stuart (1952) all arrive at a similar figure. Furthermore, surveys by the Young Publishers (1959) and Groomsbridge (1964) found that those who read most tend to obtain their books from the widest variety of sources.

Several surveys have attempted to define the correlates of reading habits. Abrams (1900) came to the conclusion that, taken separately, age, class and educational background are factors determining important correlates of the type and extent of newspaper reading; however, some very striking differences in newspaper reading habits were found to occur. For example, when these factors interact within the middle class there are, between those with higher education and those without it, differences in reading habits just as great as the broad differences between the 'average middle-class adult' and the 'average working-class adult'.

Stuart (1952) found that the average time spent on reading increased with educational level. He concluded that age, level of education and social class influence reading patterns.

In their well known research, Gray and Rogers (1956) discovered that reading competence appears to be more closely related to educational background than are reading interests and purposes. The maturity of an individual's reading interests and purposes was found to relate less to the amount of education, but more closely to the extent to which an individual's world extends beyond the range of his own immediate needs.

So the relationship between education and reading is particularly confusing. Reading competence, defined as the cognitive function of low-level understanding, is more closely related to educational background than reading interests and purposes. It is usually true that the longer a person's education the greater is likely to be his understanding of what he reads. However, this is not necessarily true of reading interests or of a variety of reading purposes. The ability to read fluently and widely is not an inevitable concomitant of success in education. Formal education is not by itself a dependable predictor of maturity in reading.

Adolescent reading

What is the extent of reading among adolescents?
Two American studies *The San Francisco Study of Children and Mass Communication* (1959) and *A Study of the Interests of Children and Youth* (1960), found that the average amount of time devoted to reading outside the school by pupils up to the ninth grade was 1.1 hours per day. Moreover the ninth grade pupils read little more than the middle grade child. Compared with television, reading was found to have relatively small appeal. Witty (1962) is in agreement, '. . . the small amount of time devoted to reading—about one hour each day—stands out in sharp contrast with the larger amount—three hours daily—given to TV'. Pugh (1969) corroborated these findings in his research among Yorkshire secondary schoolchildren. He discovered that whereas 91 per cent of his respondents watched television daily, only 14 per cent spent more than eight hours a week on reading. McCullough (1957) found that only 48 per cent of children in the top socioeconomic group reported having done some reading in their weeklong logs. Witty (1962) concluded that, '. . . the present status of reading among children is by no means satisfactory. The average child does not appear to read widely.'

The situation in Britain may not be very different. Whitehead (1971) noted that, '. . . a majority of children in each age group (i.e. ten, twelve, fourteen years) claim to have read at least one book during the previous four weeks, and the outstanding impression gained from their answers is of the remarkable diversity and variety of their book reading'. He also pointed out that there was, unsurprisingly, evidence of extensive reading of comics by the majority of children throughout the age range studied. In this he agrees with the findings of Jenkinson (1940), Alderson (1968), Pugh (1969) and Hayes (1972). Jenkinson, Pugh and Hayes also found extensive reading of newspapers.

Jenkinson (1940), in his classic British study, described three average schoolboy reading patterns per month:

1   Fourteen plus secondary—reads six books out of school and half a book in school during private reading periods.
2   Fourteen plus senior—reads four books out of school and two books in school.
3   Fifteen plus—reads five books out of school, no private reading.

Caution must always be employed in interpreting these questionnaire findings as children may well feel under some obligation to put the extent of their reading in a favourable light. However, using an indirect interview technique, Pugh (1969) found that in the two months prior to the investigation 19 per cent had read more than seven books, 12.5 per cent had read six or seven, 22.5 per cent read four or five, 26 per cent read two or three and 5 per cent read one.

What role does the school play in promoting reading?

Pugh (1971) asked the respondents where they obtained books and why they selected them. He concluded that, although the school library is of importance, teachers do not always recommend books, and when they do so their recommendations are not highly favoured by the pupils. He makes the point, 'When we split up the sample into 'avid' readers (i.e. those who had read six or more books in the last two months) and 'less eager' readers (i.e. those who had read three books or less), it appeared that teacher influence was slight in both groups. Far more surprising and suggestive is the influence of friends and of librarians.' Holbrook (1961) concluded from the figures provided in the W.H. Smith and George Harrap survey that, 'Another obvious deduction . . . is that it is the home which influences the grammar and public school child . . . whereas it is obviously the school which makes the reading habits of secondary modern school children.'

However, the evidence strongly suggests that teachers do not influence secondary school reading to the extent to which they would wish.

Which authors do pupils like best?

Jenkinson (1940) found Charles Dickens, P. G. Wodehouse, John Bunyan and R. L. Stevenson were favourite authors. Chambers (1969) quotes a teacher-librarian in a grammar school who gave H. G. Wells, Hammond Innes, John Buchan and A. Conan Doyle as favourite authors and Mrs Ray, the Leicester Children's and Youth Librarian, who listed Josephine Kamm, John Wyndham, Neville Shute and Beverly Cleary. Holbrook (1961) quoting the Smith and Harrap survey, lists W. E. Johns, Conan Doyle and Enid Blyton. Yarlott and Harpin (1970) list Ian Fleming, D. H. Lawrence, Agatha Christie and Wells. Whitehead (1971) lists Blyton, Dickens, Christie and Stevenson. Hayes (1972) found that Alfred Hitchcock, Wells, Dickens and Blyton topped the 'favourite author' and 'most read author' lists. These surveys show an unexplained constant flux in emphasis and taste within a similar age range.

What kinds of books do pupils like?

Carlsen (1967) reached the conclusion that adolescents generally choose or reject books on the actual subject-matter content of the book. He found that the three favourite types of stories were nonfiction adventure, war stories and adolescent life. Jenkinson (1940) found that adventure and detective stories were by far the most popular types of stories—a finding repeated in my research. Chambers (1969) discovered that ghost stories, animal stories, science fiction and film tie-ups were the kind of books on which young people spent their money. Fader (1966) found that social action books were the most popular followed by James Bond, war stories, humour, suspense and horror in that order. Yarlott and Harpin (1970) found humorous writing, mystery and suspense, serious novels and science fiction the most popular.

What are the 'interest' characteristics of books and readers?
Both Chambers (1969) and Mann (1969) have emphasized the prime importance of plot in motivating poor readers. Terman and Lima (1931) identified a number of factors affecting reading interests such as age, health, physical development, social environment, home training, mental ability and sex.

Norvell (1958) concluded that the elements favoured by boys included adventurous action, physical struggle, human characters, animals, humour, courage, heroism and patriotism. Paffard (1962) believed that secondary school pupils prefer literature written in easy language, dealing with themes that are relatively immature emotionally, in which they find it easy to identify themselves with the hero or heroine and in which the element of wish fulfilment is comparatively open. Carlsen (1967) found that boys liked the leading characters to be masculine; they liked a large cast of characters; a story with a setting that takes them round the world; the intrigue of much action often involving several different plots; they tended to prefer descriptions of external actions of the characters. Yarlott and Harpin (1970) found that on the whole boys tended to prefer 'masculine' writers like Fleming, Hemingway, Asimov or Forester 'who provided a strong narrative line with plenty of action and thrills'. They seldom nominated women writers. Girls were found to be especially fond of writers of their own sex, and among male writers often chose those who are credited with insight into the behaviour and personalities of women—Lawrence, Hardy and Gallico. Hayes (1972) found that excitement and sex were seen as the most popular ingredients for a 'good' book—a point emphasized by the two favourite books in the survey *Skinhead* and *Suedehead.*

Attitudes to reading in general
Pugh (1969) found that 40 per cent of his respondents expressed a positive and apparently genuine appreciation of the value and/or pleasure derived from reading, while only 12 per cent considered reading to be a waste of time. Yarlott and Harpin (1971) discovered that, while sixteen to eighteen year olds resorted to leisure reading for a variety of purposes, like adults they read books chiefly for entertainment or enjoyment. They were surprised at their own discovery, 'The preference for light reading, for books which give uncomplicated pleasure and amusement is most marked.' Hayes (1972) found that although the majority of his respondents gave reasons for and against reading, the bias was in favour of reading.

Summary
Very generally it can be seen that although reading is by no means a major activity for many schoolchildren, within the reading done there appears to be great diversity. It is possible to locate factors that influence reading choice and interest in the pupil, (both in the environment and in the reading matter). Although the teacher's suggested reading is not generally approved of by the pupils, it is interesting to note the general finding that the pupils' favourite authors are often the considered old favourites of teachers. How-

ever, this finding may not be entirely reliable as it is known that children are often unable to give the names of authors of the books which they read. A healthy sign is the wide variety of books which pupils choose to read.

The role of reading
Reading is a relatively new activity when one compares it with speaking, listening and writing and the study of reading has not as yet produced a sufficiently wide concept structure to denote the variety of activities that go on under the general term reading. Much of the educational research has concentrated on beginning reading, and while many people can read in the mechanical sense, L. E. W. Smith (1972) argues that very few, '. . . make the kind of concentrated and sensitive response that is needed to pick up all the clues and signals, and understand what is being said below the surface. To teach children to read, in this sense, should be one of the main aims of the English teacher.'

As yet the sequence of stages leading to this kind of reading is not generally agreed and this, together with a certain lack of agreement on what precisely is to be developed, may explain the lack of success in the teaching of reading in secondary education. It is important that reading should be seen by teachers as a developing but learned skill. However, skill development is not the whole of reading. As well as the skill element one must also be constantly aware that a child's school-initiated reading could be the start of a valued lifetime habit. I have found that basic reading 'competence' tends to be stressed at the secondary school level at the expense of interest and purpose (Hayes 1972).

Scherer (1966) dealing with second language teaching, emphasizes that reading and language fluency are necessary for the study of literature and should precede it. Although his work is primarily concerned with reading in foreign languages, its relevance lies in the fact that teachers of languages have a unique opportunity to observe reading skill development from the word recognition level to the fluent adult reading level. From his study he developed the concepts of 'intensive' and 'extensive' reading. He, in fact, analyses six levels of reading competence. It is in the fourth stage of reading competence, the pupil having now grasped the mechanics and basic steps of the reading process, that the two above concepts come into play. Stages five—maturity—and six—pleasure—result from the pupil's assimilation of the skills needed at previous stages, and are dependent on the pupil's ability to read, independently, at both intensive and extensive levels. It is important for teachers to differentiate between the two types of reading and to encourage both. Scherer claimed that reading education provides almost exclusively intensive reading, that is 'competence', at the expense of extensive reading, that is fluency. Witty (1965) has stated, 'In case studies one can show too, large gains in reading skills associated with wide reading based on pupil interest . . . . But the value of reading experience chosen in accordance with interest and need has been shown repeatedly in case studies to lead pupils to attain a better understanding of themselves and their social environment.' Flower (1966) has pointed out that the simplest way in which we can help the pupil's language is by developing the reading habit. He maintains that this should be done by encouraging extensive reading for the sake of content, for information and for entertainment.

The relationship between interest and reading is vital to any development of pleasurable reading. Witty (1965) came to the conclusion that lack of interest is an outstanding factor in the failure of both children and adults to read widely and well. Yarlott and Harpin (1971) discuss the interest element in teaching literature in the conclusion of their report:

> But all too frequently, it seems, our present methods of teaching and examining English Literature fail to take into account the 'consumers' response to the subject. There is a tendency to prescribe what 'ought' to be read without any regard to how the prescription relates to the pupil's immediate interests and concerns and to his own reading preferences.

Teachers' attitudes are of vital importance in that they affect their own conception of their role, their opinion of the reading being done, and also their understanding or lack of understanding of the cultural activities and interests of the children. Children tend to adopt quite different approaches to private reading and to school reading. The good teacher can, as both Fader and Flower point out, by beginning with the child and his special interests and needs, make school reading as relevant to the child as his private reading. Fader (1966) says that pupils 'must be met where they are before they can be led to where they should be'. The sentiment is echoed by Flower (1966), 'The first need in all our work is to bring the literature we study into a context which makes some kind of sense to the student.'

The need is to leave the game of 'Let's Pretend' described by Postman and Weingarter (1971) and to play a new game, the aim of which is purposeful reading for pleasure and interest. Holt (1971) concludes, 'This is exactly what reading should be and in school so seldom is—an exciting, joyous adventure.' Carlsen (1967) points out that the good reader is a person who enjoys reading and that a child's reading skill will grow in direct proportion to the degree of success and enjoyment he finds in books.

The inevitable conclusion is that the teacher can dictate success and failure. The attention given by teachers to what a pupil reads has proved, by its exaggerated emphasis on 'quality', damaging in the extreme to the quantity of a pupil's reading. Bamberger (1971) concluded, 'The best methods are of no avail though when the most essential attribute is lacking: the genuine interest of the teacher . . . it is the teacher who determines whether reading teaching is successful or not.' Robinson (1956) in stressing the importance of the interest factor in reading placed the responsibility firmly on the teacher in ascertaining and utilizing interest. Alderson (1968) argues that the material given to children in schools is often too far from their general experience and interests. Dismissal, however well intentioned, of much of what children enjoy in reading and premature attempts to substitute our 'literary heritage' may well serve only to aberrate children from 'good' literature.

Conclusion

Reading has two sides, skills and interests, and it is the school's role to concern itself with both aspects. The concern of the English teacher should be to provide the pupil with a basis for his choice and appreciation of reading matter. This can best be done by beginning where the pupils are and leading them outwards. It would seem to be a waste of time to teach literary critical techniques to children who do not wish to read the books being studied. Children must be encouraged to read profusely and widely so that interest is developed in preparation of informed literary analysis. The distinction between skill and appreciation must be stressed here. They are distinct but related aspects of reading. Reading is not only a linguistic process but also demands an evaluative component.

The research cited shows that some reading is being done, but that it is generally fragmentary and misguided. Many adolescents read but seem to read in spite of school. This situation has to be remedied and the main onus appears to lie with the individual teachers to reconsider their attitudes, purposes and methods.

There is little doubt that reading is considered to be a valuable activity by the majority of adolescents. However, it is an activity that requires comparatively more effort for enjoyment than other valued interests. It is the teacher's role to give reading an interest and purpose as well as to cultivate competence and critical literary reading. Reading should both be intensive and extensive, but primarily it should be enjoyable.

References

ABRAMS, M. (n.d.) *Education, Social Class and Reading of Newspapers* London: Institute of Practitioners in Advertising

ALDERSON, C. (1968) *Magazines Teenagers Read* London: Pergamon Press

BAMBERGER, R. (1971) *Lese—Erziehung* Vienna: Leinmüller

CARLSEN, G. R. (1967) *Books and the Teenage Reader* New York: Harper and Row

CHAMBERS, A. (1969) *The Reluctant Reader* London: Pergamon Press

CENTRAL ADVISORY COUNCIL FOR EDUCATION (1959) *15 to 18* (Crowther Report) London: HMSO

FADER, D. (1966) *Hooked on Books* London: Pergamon Press

FLOWER, F. (1966) *Language and Education* London: Longman

GRAY, W. S. and ROGERS, B. (1956) *Maturity in Reading* Chicago: University of Chicago Press

GROOMSBRIDGE, B. (1964) *The Londoner and his Library* London: The Research Institute for Consumer Affairs

HAYES, E. J. (1972) *Reading in the Secondary School* Unpublished BEd thesis

HOLBROOK, D. (1961) *English for Maturity* London: Cambridge University Press

HOLT, J. (1971) *The Underachieving School* Harmondsworth: Penguin

INTERNATIONAL PUBLISHING CORPORATION (1966) 'Interests in sports, hobbies and leisure activities' in D. H. Mann and J. L. Burgoyne (Eds) (1969) *Books and Reading* London: Andre Deutsch

JENKINSON, A. J. (1940) *What Do Boys and Girls Read?* London: Methuen

MANN, D. H. and BURGOYNE, J. L. (Eds) (1969) *Books and Reading* London: Andre Deutsch

McCULLOUGH, C. (1957) A log of children's out of school activities *The Elementary School Journal* LVIII, December

NORTHWESTERN UNIVERSITY AND OFFICE OF EDUCATION, US DEPARTMENT OF HEALTH, EDUCATION AND WELFARE (1960) *A Study of the Interests of Children and Youth* Washington: Government Printing Office

NORVELL, G. W. (1958) *What Boys and Girls Like to Read* New Jersey: Silver Burdett

PAFFARD, M. K. (1962) The teaching of English Literature in secondary schools *Educational Research* 4, 5

POSTMAN, N. and WEINGARTER, C. (1971) *Teaching as a Subversive Activity* Harmondsworth: Penguin

PUGH, A. K. (1969) Some neglected aspects of reading in the secondary school *Reading* 3, 3

PUGH, A. K. (1971) Secondary school reading: obstacles to profit and delight *Reading* 5, 1

ROBINSON, H, (1956) *Developing Permanent Interest in Reading* Chicago: University of Chicago Press

SCHERER, G. A. (1966) 'Programmed second language reading' in G. Matthieu (Ed) *Advances in the Teaching of Modern Languages* London: Pergamon Press

SMITH, L. E. W. (1972) *Towards a New English Curriculum* London: Dent

STANFORD INSTITUTE FOR COMMUNICATION RESEARCH (1959) *The San Francisco Study of Children and Mass Communication* Stanford: California

STUART, A. (1952) Reading habits in three London boroughs *Journal of Documentation* 8, 1

TERMAN, L. M. and LIMA, M. (1931) *Children's Reading: A Guide for Parents and Teachers* New York: Appleton

WHITEHEAD, E. S. (1971) *Schools Council Research into Children's Reading Habits* University of Sheffield Institute of Education: Press Release

WITTY, P. (1962) 'Mass media and reading' in J. A. Figurel (Ed) *Challenge and Experiment in Reading* New York: Scholastic Magazines

WITTY, P. (1965) 'Studies of children's interests—a brief summary' in W. B. Barbe *Teaching Reading: Selected Materials* New York: Oxford University Press

YARLOTT, G. and HARPIN, W. S. (1970 and 1971) 1000 Responses to
    English Literature: 1 and 2 *Educational Research* 13, 1 and 2
YOUNG PUBLISHERS (1959) Books in London 1959 *Books* Jan-Feb

19 Assessing reading progress in secondary schools

D. S. Macleod

The problem and the context of discussion

Despite the movement of expert opinion towards a definition of reading as 'a long term developmental process of increasing complexity' (UKRA representation to Committee of Inquiry into Reading, 1972) provision for the systematic development and assessment of advanced reading skills in secondary school lags considerably behind provision made in primary school with regard to initial skills.

There are, certainly, special difficulties besetting the secondary school:

1. subdivision of the curriculum into frequently exclusive specialist subject areas
2. unawareness on the part of subject specialists of the continuing nature of reading development
3. lack of definition of responsibility for teaching and assessing reading.

As a result the secondary pupil is often ill-equipped to cope with the varying demands of increasingly specialist study, and assessment of his reading progress founders on questions of first principle.

Possible solutions to some of these difficulties are anticipated here in the context of a current research project into the teaching of reading in Scottish schools, financed by the Social Science Research Council. The older of two samples, whose selection details follow, are being followed from seventh and final year primary to third year secondary stage, age range in Scotland eleven to twelve years to fourteen to fifteen years. At the moment, summer 1973, the sample has been assessed over one school session 1972-73 while aged eleven to twelve years i.e. comparable in age with pupils now completing first year secondary stage in England. It will be seen therefore that assessment details of the sample have a double relevance: in Scotland they provide an indication of the kind of pupils arriving in secondary school in autumn 1973, while in England they offer comparison with first year secondary pupils.

Selection and testing of sample

Despite changing characteristics due to administrative reorganization, a sample of fourteen secondary schools was selected according to certain criteria to include as comprehensive a range of types of school as possible, although not necessarily a proportionately representative range. Criteria were: size of roll, type of course offered, whether grant-aided or local authority including Roman Catholic, and socioeconomic environment.

From the selected secondary schools, fifty-eight primary 'feeder' schools were identified, covering the secondary catchment area. The Edinburgh Reading Test Stage 3 was administered to all ninety-seven final year primary classes in these schools in autumn, 1972, average age at date of test 11 years 4 months. This measure of initial reading level of the sample is to be complemented at the end of the three year period of enquiry by the administration of a further reading test. This will provide a measure of reading attainment progress in terms of skills seen to be relevant to this period of the sample's education. Meanwhile, with the class and its teacher as the unit of investigation, factors affecting reading progress are being explored.

Textbook readability

In discussion with class teachers of the sample, a wide variety of reading materials was found to be in use. The question arose whether these materials and the skills they demand related in any way to materials used subsequently in secondary school; and to what extent was it legitimate to regard teaching of reading in secondary school as a continuation from primary school.

It was found that, although often published in numbered series, little objective measure of the readability of materials was available to allow teachers in the sample to substantiate intuitive choice of text for class use. Comparative data was seen as useful in helping to match a text more accurately to the assessed ability of the pupil and in making available information concerning a wide range of materials to the busy class teacher.

Selection of the means of objective measurement of readability concentrated on the existing range of formulae although their significant limitations (cf. Reid 1972) include neglect of syntactical complexity, thought to be more central to text difficulty than lexical range. However, an easily applied measure was sought to establish comparative data for a wide range of texts which could be continuously extended. For this reason McLaughlin's SMOG readability formula was selected and applied to a representative selection of the most commonly used readers to which the sample, while aged eleven to twelve, has been exposed. It is important to stress that the SMOG reading grade is that which a person must have reached if he is to understand fully the text assessed. This contrasts with the Dale and Chall formula which accepts 50 per cent success as the criterion. As a result, acknowledged by McLaughlin 1969, the SMOG gradings are generally two grades higher than those given by the considerably more time-consuming Dale-Chall (see Table 1 page 159).

On this evidence the above reading materials in use with the eleven to twelve year old sample require a range of reading ability of five years. Do secondary reading materials compare in scope, and is the SMOG readability technique applicable to such materials? The books examined above were of the prose extract type, both fiction and nonfiction. They

Table 1

Series	% use with sample	Reader analysed	Readability grade
First Aid in English	24	Bk E	SMOG 7-8
SRA Reading Laboratory	20	IIC	(Dale-Chall 5-6)
SRA Pilot Library			
Good Company	4	Bk 5	SMOG 8-9
Swift Reader	5	Bks 4 and 5	(Dale-Chall 6-7)
New Worlds to Conquer	7	Bks 4 and 5	SMOG 10-11
			(Dale-Chall 8-9)

often rose in readability level from opening to final page. Comparable extract anthologies are used in secondary school: English interpretation passages, language translation exercises, samples of historical documents. An increased amount of continuous prose is in use, accessible to the formula. Problems arise, however, with, for example, trigonometry theorems, accounts of chemistry experiments laced with equations or similar materials with nonverbal content. Some relative means of assessing reading difficulty should be found to include the wide range of types of teaching materials in secondary schools.

Extension of readability measurement is also proposed to include reading material current with the sample outside the school day, to establish relative difficulty levels and the relationship of this to reading progress.

Out of school reading habits

An investigation was planned to establish the relationship, if any, between the amount, diversity and source of reading done out of school by the sample to their measured level of reading attainment. This would reveal the kinds of reading habits with which the sample would arrive at secondary school. An inquiry into how the secondary school copes with such a situation is planned, together with the readministration of the questionnaire after two years of secondary schooling to detect any developments.

A questionnaire, included on page 161, was constructed for administration by the classteacher. This took place in June 1973, when each pupil in the sample was asked to recall reading out of school hours during the preceding week. This recall of source, diversity and amount was recognized as open to overestimate. Nevertheless, for purposes of coarse comparison, a pupil reading more than one of a given type of literature was taken to be a keen reader of that type.

Small classes under ten strong were excluded from assessment of returns which indicated a positive relationship between the amount of nonfiction and, especially, fiction read out of school and reading attainment (see Table 2 below). Consumption of ephemeral literature was consistently

Table 2 High reading consumption related to mean reading score

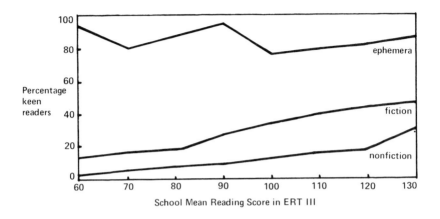

high, apparently without relation to reading attainment (see Table 3 below for most popular ephemera by type). An enormous variety of other publications read by less than 2 per cent of the sample figured in returns. Consumption of lighter ephemera was consistently higher than that of the more demanding ephemera.

Table 3

% age readership in sample	comics	newspapers	magazines
18		Daily Record	
16		Sunday Post	Jackie
13	Dandy/Beano		
10	Beezer	Daily Express	
8	Bunty		Diana
7		Scotsman	Music Star
6		Local	
3		newspapers	Look In
2			World of Wonder
			Look & Learn

On the other items, increased use of available sources of reading material was related to higher reading attainment, as was a greater amount of out of school reading assigned or stimulated by the teacher.

The information which can be gleaned from such an enquiry is seen to have considerable relevance to the needs of the secondary pupil to:

160

1   establish awareness of the reading habits of the pupil beyond the classroom
2   test preconceived notions about the consequences of the reading habits of the over twelves in the light of relationships between consumption of different kinds and quantities of literature and reading attainment
3   relate the readability of classroom and personal reading materials
4   tap the reading motivation of the pupils
5   establish awareness of the reading environment of the pupil outside school.

Questionnaire: Reading out of school hours

Write your name: Your class:
Today's date: Your school:

Here are some questions about what you have read *out of school hours during the past seven days*. Answer by *underlining* or *writing on the line* where you are asked.

1   Underline one or more of the sentences below to show where your reading material during the past week came from:
    (a) I did not read a book, comic or newspaper out of school hours
    (b) What I read belonged to me, or to someone in my family, or to a friend
    (c) It belonged to my teacher or my school
    (d) It belonged to a library outside school

2   Underline any of the things below which you have done out of school hours during the past week:
    (a) preparing your reading for school
    (b) looking up information for a project or for other class work
    (c) reading for pleasure about something which interested you in school
    (d) none of these things

3   Underline *none, one* or *more than one* below to show what *kinds* of reading you have done during the past week. Then *write on the line* briefly, what it was about:

    Books: nonfiction
    (a) None
    (b) One
    (c) More than one

    Books: fiction
    (b) None

F   161

(b) One
(c) More than one

Comics, newspapers or magazines
(a) None
(b) One
(c) More than one

Transition from primary to secondary school reading
In discussion with sample secondary schools desirable practices have been
put forward with regard to preparation of pupils for secondary entry:

1 establishment of open communication between a secondary school
  and its primary feeders
2 transmission of detailed records of the pupils' reading progress
4 teaching visits by secondary staff to meet primary pupils on familiar
  ground
5 joint discussion of transition pupils with a view to provision of remedial
  help
6 involvement of parents, family and older secondary pupils in making
  the transition from primary to secondary a natural progression.

Thus the needs of the whole child are acknowledged in the effort to
safeguard and promote his reading effectiveness in this vital period of
change.

Assessing reading skills in secondary school
The limited number of standardized reading tests for the secondary pupil
measure a restricted range of skills; word recognition, vocabulary, comprehension and reading speed. Details of British and American tests are
given in UKRA Bibliography No 2, *The Assessment of Reading Skills.*
Different styles of reading are evolving, however, in the course of
secondary education. It is desirable to extend assessment to progress in
such skills as:

1 general critical appraisal of reading matter
2 reading to establish the gist of a passage
3 skimming to select information according to prescribed criteria
4 close, detailed study of intricate or logically difficult text
5 perception of different styles of written language, using linguistic and
  content cues
6 reading beyond explicit information to draw on areas of inference.

Apart from statistical requirements, the difficulty in constructing items
which test these skills lies in selecting a passage of practicable yet valid
length which demands the adoption of a particular style of reading. The

recurring general comprehension passage of English textbooks illustrates the difficulty of departing from conventional forms. There can be little doubt, however, of the pressing need for a more broadly based standardized test or battery of tests to assess reading development in the secondary school.

Responsibility within the secondary school

The particular difficulties, mentioned in the opening paragraph, which impede the teaching and assessment of reading as a developmental process in secondary school provide starting points for reform:

1 There must be recognition of the need for the pupil to acquire advanced reading skills which may partake of specialist subjects or cut across conventional subject boundaries.

2 Pre- and in-service training opportunities should be made available to broaden the secondary specialist's conception of the role of reading in relation to his subject and to the curriculum in general.

3 A responsibility structure should be established in the secondary school for the development and assessment of reading, the main weight of responsibility lying with reading specialists whose functions could include:

    i   establishment of consensus on relevant general and specialist reading skills to be taught

    ii   coordination of records and assessment procedures, and of the system of reference to remedial services

    iii transmission of reading research findings.

References

ALDERSON, C. (1968) *Magazines Teenagers Read* London: Pergamon

CENTRAL COMMITTEE ON ENGLISH (1967) *English in Secondary School: Early Stages* London: HMSO

FARR, R. (1970) *Measurement and Evaluation of Reading* New York: Harcourt, Brace and World

GILLILAND, J. (1972) *Readability* London: University of London Press

KEMBLE, B. (1971) *Fit to Teach* London: Hutchinson

MELNICK, A. and MERRITT, J. (1972) *Reading Today and Tomorrow* London: University of London Press/Oxford University Press

MORRISON, A. and MACINTYRE, D. (1969) *Teachers and Teaching* Harmondsworth: Penguin

OLSON, A. V. and AMES, W. S. (1970) *Teaching Reading Skills in Secondary Schools: Readings* London: International Textbook Company

PUGH, A. K. (1971) Secondary school reading: obstacles to profit and delight *Reading*, 5, 1

PUGH, A. K. (1972) 'Reading in the secondary school: an unassumed responsibility' in V. Southgate (Ed) *Literacy at all Levels* London: Ward Lock Educational

REID, J. F. (1972) *Reading: Problems and Practices* London: Ward Lock Educational

STREVENS, P. D. (1965) *Papers in Language and Language Teaching* London: Oxford University Press

UKRA. (1972) *Evidence to Committee of Inquiry into Reading and the Use of English in Schools*

WALSH, J. H. (1965) *Teaching English* London: Heinemann

WHITEHEAD, F. (1968) *The Disappearing Dais* London: Chatto and Windus

20 Illiteracy—an assessment of the problems and the prospects for its remediation

Philip Ralph

The extent of the problem

If one is a teacher one tends to move in circles in which illiteracy is unlikely to be a major problem. Most of our relatives and friends are either professional people or those doing jobs which require good intelligence and skill of a high order; therefore apart from an occasional so-called dyslexic, a brain damaged child or one of the mental defectives who are occasionally born to parents of better than average intelligence, our personal knowledge of the problem is minimal. Also, as one can readily understand, in a literate society the illiterate takes such steps as he can to disguise his deficiency.

Some of the ploys used are simple like 'I cannot see without my glasses' said by someone who has never seen an optician in his life. Others will arrange to have their wages paid into a joint account in a bank so that their mates do not discover that they cannot read or write and the bank staff do not notice either because after the conclusion of the initial business of opening the account, the wife withdraws the money. It has been known, when documents are being handed round to a group of people, for the illiterate to put on a wonderful act of apparently intently studying the document rather than show himself up. It has been my experience that most illiterates are very sensitive indeed regarding their shortcomings. Many of them are willing to make considerable financial or other sacrifices in order to acquire a modicum of reading and writing ability. Teachers who, like myself, have taught senior ESNs (i.e. children aged fourteen to sixteen with an intelligence quotient or reading quotient below about 75 or 80) will know that some are able to read reasonably well when they leave, whilst others can 'get by' on a bare minimum of practical, everyday 'bread and butter' words.

However, just a few members of our society (and I think I ought to emphasize that it is a residual problem—quite a small percentage when compared to the whole community) are illiterate and feel very intensely their inadequacy and inferiority. You have only to meet some of them to realize how sensitive they are. So let us have a closer look at the problem.

One morning when I was preparing this paper I read a report of the Merseyside Chamber of Commerce, which was addressed to all employers in that area, drawing their attention to the liability of hundreds of teenage workers to sustain serious injury at work because of their inability to read and write. It was stated that because of increasing illiteracy (their words) many boys and girls miss warning notices and instructions on dangerous machinery. It was said that a number of firms had had to either sack or retrain many young people because they could not read or write or do simple arithmetic. The Chamber of Commerce spokesman is reported to have said (and I quote) that 'there was not enough coordination and liaison between headmasters when children moved from junior schools to secondary schools and even further down the line from infant schools to juniors'. He said that this lead to youngsters having a very unsettled education and that not enough attention was paid to the three Rs.

The group training officer of Pilkingtons the glass manufacturers has said, 'Many youngsters here cannot read and this indeed worries us from the safety point of view; they just do not know what warning notices say, but we find it so very difficult to find out who the illiterate people are.'

There are social problems too. How do you communicate with Mum and Dad and the boy or girl friend when you are away from home and they are not on the phone? How do you fill in the multiplicity of forms which seem to be inseparable from normal life in the twentieth century? How do you know which tablets to take from the medicine cabinet in the bathroom or how many or how often, especially if you forgot to ask the doctor who gave you the prescription, or if you are taking a proprietary article?

It is perhaps a little surprising but I am officially informed that an illiterate may obtain a driving licence provided he can read numbers and sign his name, and that someone is prepared to teach him his Highway Code; but how difficult it must be to get around the countryside if, because one cannot read direction signs, one has to be continually asking directions orally.

This is perhaps almost enough about practical difficulties but it is necessary to point out the need to read entrance and exit or in and out, up and down and so on. Some of you may have seen an amusing cartoon (amusing to us) of an irate umbrella-waving lady chasing a young man up the steps and away from a door marked *Ladies.*

We have just been thinking of the practical aspects of the problem, but what about the psychological ones? There is the frustration of trying to exist in an environment in which most things one has to do and which are possibly stretching one to the limit of one's intelligence become twice as difficult or perhaps impossible because of illiteracy.

One wonders how many intelligent and literate people have resorted to either violent actions or words when a screw-head has broken off or the lead of the vacuum cleaner has gone wrong just at an inopportune moment? The frustration felt by the illiterate is much worse than this and in many cases is manifested in violence towards our society which seems to the illiterate to provide such a hostile environment. An illiterate's sense of inferiority also shows itself in various other attempts to prove himself. Some of these are laudable like making superhuman efforts to shine at some sport or pastime; others are less praiseworthy like indulgence in non-violent forms of delinquency.

An example of this is a boy who had reached the age of thirteen without being able to read a single word. The boy was accepted as a pupil by a remedial specialist who decided to put aside all usual methods and, after enquiring into the boy's interests, taught him to read on Vauxhall car catalogues. The first words he learnt to recognize were clutch, gear-box and differential. This boy's attitude to life completely changed, his frustration and sense of inferiority were removed. He had been the most insolent, dishonest and generally insubordinate pupil the school had known for many years but after specialist attention he won two school prizes in one year—one for best progress and the other for courtesy and good behaviour.

Remediation

Personal experience as a teacher of educationally subnormal children and as a remedial specialist in ordinary schools has shown that most children can be taught to read. The innately dull can, with sympathetic help and by stretching their inadequate mental equipment to the full, learn to read to a limited extent. The true remedial subject who has failed because of deprivation of some kind such as poor home environment, bad health, emotional problems, because his teachers have failed to make allowances for poor sight or hearing, or for a variety of other reasons, can become a perfectly normal reader once his difficulties have been removed or compensated for. A few pupils with intelligence quotients somewhere around the fifty mark will have reached the mental age of eight by the time they leave school at sixteen and are just ready to make progress when they are due to leave school. (We know that intelligence tests are not the precise indicators that we once thought them to be but they are still a most useful guide if used sensibly.)

The problem of illiteracy is a residual one in that probably less than 1 per cent leave school completely illiterate but if you are one of the illiterates and either you are sensitive about it or the illiteracy holds you back throughout your life it is a very serious matter indeed. For instance, it can often prevent progress in the person's chosen occupation. He finds himself working below capacity doing unskilled jobs instead of skilled ones. He is the first to become unemployed when jobs are scarce. It creates difficulties when he tries to express himself in conversation and in understanding or giving instructions. Illiteracy is also a serious problem in another aspect of our national life. It is perhaps sufficient to say that all of our prisons and borstals have to make special provision for their illiterates who make up much more than 1 per cent of their population. This is, of course, another measure of the seriousness of the problem.

Before going on to discuss treatment it would perhaps be opportune to qualify the forgoing remarks with a few definitions of illiteracy. *From a UNESCO Committee:* 'A person is considered *literate* who can both read with understanding and write a short simple statement on his everyday life'; 'A person is considered *semiliterate* who can read with understanding but not write a short simple statement on his everyday life.' Professor Grey in the UNESCO publication *The Teaching of Reading and Writing* introduces the term 'functional literacy' for the person who has 'acquired the knowledge and skills in reading and writing which enable him to engage effectively in all those activities in which literacy is normally assumed in his culture or group'.

The armed forces of our country describe an illiterate as one with a reading age of under seven years and a semiliterate as one with a reading age of under nine years; the former being 1 per cent of the population, the latter a further 2.6 per cent but it is problematical whether this same proportion would be found in civilian society.

Probably one way in which to illustrate approximately what these reading ages signify is to refer to a series of readers such as *Adventures in Reading* which begins at a reading age of six and a half to seven years, and its counterpart *New Adventures in Reading* with an approx. reading age of nine years. Examination of these will help us to visualize the extent of the problem but a valuable exercise would be a consideration of what we consider to be the absolute minimum needs of any person who is to be able to exist in our society with support from others and without reference to others in matters which require the visual communication skills of reading and writing.

What are these minimum needs for travelling to and from work, safety at work, shopping, filling in forms, basic needs in the home, minimum communication purposes, for social prestige and self-esteem? How much does the semiliterate suffer as a result of being unable adequately to read the paper or any form of literature?

Teaching the illiterate and semiliterate

Teaching techniques can always be improved and electronic gadgetry can also be improved and made more sophisticated but there is already available adequate 'know-how' and equipment for helping the people we are considering. The National Association for Remedial Education has within its ranks a great many people who could guide and support teachers willing to undertake the teaching of illiterates but perhaps a more important consideration is the need to prevent illiteracy occurring.

Factors within the education system which contribute to the failure to eradicate illiteracy are inadequate teaching at the infant stage; over-enthusiasm which causes some teachers to force children to try to read before they are ready; inadequate knowledge of the principles behind the learning of reading skills especially amongst teachers in the middle and secondary schools. It is suggested that there are inadequate means of passing on information on pupils from one stage of education to the next; that there is a lack of awareness of the problem amongst teachers of other subjects and thus a failure to bring to the notice of the remedial department children who are still failing in reading. Then there are the perennial problems of oversized classes and lack of money.

It appears that a very strong case can be made for a marrying together of the bodies of expertise within UKRA and NARE and the initiation of a strong drive towards the elimination of the problem. No easy overnight solutions will be apparent but this is a matter which should be tackled with some urgency.

We must take what action we can to prevent illiteracy whilst the child is still within the school system, but some pupils will, for various reasons, still need help after they have left. The Russell Report appears to have created a favourable climate for the continuing education of less-able pupils after statutory school leaving age, thus there should be no insurmountable problems in the way of setting up a service or organization which would (given the necessary financial backing, of course) be able to deal with illiteracy in the postschool years. This would deal with those mentioned earlier who seem to only have reached the necessary maturity for reading just at the time when they are leaving school and some of those who have failed for other reasons.

Remedial teaching of any kind is impossible unless the pupils can be taught either in very small groups or singly. In most cases illiterates will need to be taught on a one to one basis for at least some of the time. It would manifestly be quite impossible to do this for financial reasons even if the large number of teachers with the necessary expertise could be made available. It seems inevitable, therefore, that a large number of volunteer helpers will be needed if progress is to be made. Experience has shown that successful work with illiterates can be done provided the volunteers are professionally trained and supervised. One assumes that this work would largely take place in the technical colleges and evening institutes but some could well be done in the pupil's own home.

As previously mentioned, suitable teaching methods are available but they will need to be adapted to suit the needs of the older, sensitive and embarrassed pupil. Likewise texts of books must be written in the vocabulary of the older pupil, even if, in the initial stages, they make use of slang and common 'with it' terminology.

Providing the facilities

There would be a great need, during the initial stages, to proceed with great caution. The work would need to be well planned and to show that those responsible had much to offer otherwise the pupil, after experiencing failure once again, could well retire into his shell for ever. Courses would need to be carefully tailored to suit the individual. One might, for instance, have coming along a former pupil of an SSN school who could, possibly, do no more than learn a very few utility words. Others might well be able to acquire true literacy.

Careful consideration would need to be given to the venue. Would our prospective pupil be put off by an imposing and impersonal technical college? Would he prefer not to be seen going to a building near his own locality when others might know the purpose of his visits? Would a homely old fashioned primary school be a better place? The teaching would obviously need to be undertaken or at least supervised by specialist teaching, but experience has shown that intelligent volunteers can do a good job. How would such volunteers be located and trained? How much training should they be given and where? Would the professional organizations be against the use of volunteers on the grounds of 'dilution'? Who would provide the money? Would the pupil be asked to contribute? If the teaching is not done at a technical college or evening institute who is to do the administration chores? These are just a few of the problems.

Publicity for facilities

Having provided the water we have to lead the horse to its source before he can drink. How does one publicize anything amongst illiterates except by word of mouth? Perhaps the expansion of local radio will be able to make a contribution here. It would certainly be one form of publicity as also would regional television. Welfare and social workers, youth club leaders, probation officers and others who similarly come into contact with possible clients could be made more aware of the results of illiteracy, the need to eliminate it and to publicize by word of mouth such facilities as are available. Advertisements could, one imagines, be directed to the literate asking them to tactfully draw the attention of any of their illiterate acquaintances to the available tuition.

It appears that this relatively small but nonetheless important problem can only be tackled if all the available expertise is mustered and adequate finance made available. UKRA and NARE could each contribute a great deal of the expertise and, working in conjunction, could organize a real drive towards the elimination of illiteracy. Perhaps if we can show that it can be done the finance will be forthcoming.

21 Reading-for-learning—the anatomy of a research project

Laurie Thomas, Sheila Augstein and Nicholas Farnes

The shape of the project
The project can be thought to have had four main phases. These overlapped and were not as conceptually distinct as this report might appear to make them.

Phase 1 (1962-65)
A study of how undergraduates cope with their learning tasks led us to identify reading as one of the skills which students are not able to develop as a flexible and effective tool for learning. An exploratory study identified a number of questions which we went on to examine in Phase 2.

Phase 2 (1964-70)
Some five to six years of basic and applied research activity enabled us to explore these questions and a number of others in some depth. The subjects were young adults studying A level, undergraduates and a few graduates. The early work concentrated on recording strategies in reading combined with the evaluation of learning outcomes. This shed some interesting light on different examining methods. The reading recorder, flow diagram technique and taxonomy of purposes were gradually developed over this period into effective tools for heightening a person's awareness of the process of his or her reading. The final study in this phase demonstrated that students could be enabled to change their previously fixated strategies of reading.

Phase 3 (1968-72)
The model of the process of reading-for-learning which was generated by the work in phase 2 served as a basis on which to develop a series of courses in colleges of education, in Brunel, in technical colleges and in polytechnics. The powerful evidence was collected to show:

1   that the techniques could be used to help people become aware of how they read-for-learning.
2   that they could use this awareness to:
    (a)   become more varied and flexible in their strategies and tactics
    (b)   improve the effectiveness of any one tactic
    (c)   explore which tactics, for them, most effectively achieved those learning purposes which they wished to pursue.

3   that people who improved in their use of reading as a learning skill
    within a course showed significant and often startling improvements
    in subsequent academic performance. This improvement was main-
    tained over a two-year period.

Phase 4 (1970–)
This phrase is an attempt to develop and disseminate the tools, procedures
and findings of phase 3. Contributions have been made to an Open University postexperience course on Reading Development. A series of TV video-
tapes are available from Brunel. We have taken the techniques into secondary and primary schools and this pilot work looks quite promising. We
are developing learning workshops. Our current research preoccupation is
with the process of conducting an 'education conversation'. In such conversations the tools and techniques which we have developed are used to
generate a dialogue between learner and teacher. The nature of this dialogue
is such as to encourage the learner to become more aware of his processes
of reading, his purpose in reading and to evaluate his own learning performance. This enables him to become more self-organized and to accept
responsibility for learning to learn. When successful this produces a dis-
continuity in his approach to academic activities. Given a life-style in which
academic learning plays a central part, these improvements in learning skill
can change the parameters of all subsequent academic performance.

An introduction: the method of reporting
In this paper we have attempted to describe the purposes and experiences
which we have had in developing a project concerned with 'reading-for-
learning'. Our reasons for choosing this rather personal mode are twofold.
First, we see ourselves as teachers who want to know how to encourage
students to develop their own learning skills and to use these skills in
achieving their own learning purposes. Second, and for us more important,
this method of reporting allows us to illustrate what, amongst ourselves,
we have come to talk about as the 'conversational' mode in research. This
is not a question of social chit-chat, nor is it a question of one person
chatting up another. On the contrary we are concerned with serious understanding, with developing techniques by which a person can come to
appreciate the nature of his own learning processes, and with techniques
by which a teacher can encourage students to take over this self-organized
view of learning for themselves.
    We have, therefore, felt that it would be more useful to other teachers
if we report our work as it happened, rather than wrapping it up in the
paraphernalia of 'science'. Not that we haven't expended considerable
energy in developing rigorous methods and in generating evidence about
their educational effectiveness—we have. But in reporting our findings we
would like to separate the finickity questions of reliability and validity
from the direct appeal to you about 'how right' our approach feels in the
light of your own commonsense and experience as teachers.

The beginning: how the project originated

A series of exploratory studies of how undergraduates cope with the learning opportunities offered to them produced very little in the form of concrete results. But it did identify a series of questions about 'learning to learn', 'self-organization in learning' and 'personal growth' which have preoccupied the members of The Centre for the Study of Human Learning at Brunel University from then on. Laurie Thomas was lecturer in the psychology department at that time. Nicholas Farnes was one of the 'guinea pig' undergraduates and Sheila Augstein, who joined as a research assistant, was an experienced teacher of biology who had become disenchanted with successfully cramming A level students.

Interviews with students showed that even comparatively successful students rely on very limited and habitual methods of learning. These students were only vaguely aware of how they learned, and found it difficult consciously to vary their methods; they became bewildered and anxious when faced with situations where their methods were ineffective.

One problem which we identified was that of how to describe the process of learning as it takes place in the 'real world' e.g. in a lecture, in a seminar, in the library or over coffee.

Our efforts to describe the tactics and strategies of learning included one very exploratory study of how people learn by reading. We selected passages, each of about 3,000 words, from a book on Roman history, a book on psychotherapy, and a book on cybernetics. We typed each paragraph of each passage on a separate sheet of paper and made them up into booklets. Having numbered the pages of each booklet we asked students to read them in order to learn what the passage was about. They were told that they could go on reading until they were satisfied. We sat with stopwatches recording how long it took a subject to read each page (i.e. paragraph) and we also recorded the order in which the paragraphs were read. We then asked the reader to set a series of test questions which they felt would thoroughly examine whether someone else had learned all they could by reading the same passage. This gave us a measure of how the student had defined the learning task to himself. They varied greatly in the type of question they asked. Some were entirely preoccupied with detailed facts, others wanted summary-type essay answers while a few wanted the reader to extrapolate what he had read to new and novel questions or situations (e.g. how many men did Vitellus have? how did Vitellus fight the battle of Tronk? how would you have fought the battle of Tronk had you been replacing Vitellus?)

They also varied in how they read the passage. However, the majority read it once through from beginning to end. Others backtracked and skipped about among the paragraphs.

This simple experiment raised a number of questions and revealed the need for us to develop an interrelated group of new techniques.

The questions were:

1   What is a particular reader's view of effective learning?

2   How do readers' views differ and relate?
3   Do your views of what constitutes effective learning relate to how you read the text? If so, how?
4   Does the way in which you read the text relate to what you learn from it? If so, how?
5   Does the structure of meanings in a text influence how you read it? If so, how?

In order to explore question 5 we began to try to chart the meanings of the three passages visually.

Thus in this first experiment we identified the need for the tools which we have subsequently developed and attempted to use:

1   a method for recording exactly how a student reads a text
2   a method for exploring how a reader defines his learning purpose
3   a method for describing the structures of meanings which are thought to be contained by the words on the page.

The spade-work: developing the concepts, tools and techniques

The first move in this phase of the project was to develop a *machine which would record* within a few lines where a person was looking at a text and how long he spent on each line. This machine (1965) proved unreliable and we lost half our records in the early experiments which we did with it. But after a number of revisions and new designs (1970) we ended up with a reliable, efficient and relatively cheap device.

The first experiment using the early machine involved A level biology students in reading three chapters from Darwin's *Origin of Species*. Apart from finding that the reading of one chapter could take anything from twenty minutes to over three hours, the immediate result of this work was to show that people used widely different strategies and tactics in reading and produced widely different learning performances. The strategies were made up with combinations of smooth, item and search reading tactics as shown in Figure 1 below. However within the rather patchy evidence provided by these records which survived people appeared to be very consistent in the way they read. Over 90 per cent read all three chapters in the same way, although differing widely from each other.

At the end of this experiment we asked each reader to write a summary of what they had read. The problem of evaluating the summaries led us to develop a scoring system based on Bloom's *Taxonomy of Educational Objectives* which provides a hierarchical description of learning achievements. This development was the basis for the subsequent *hierarchical systems for describing purposes*.

This experiment was followed up in various ways. One way was to divide subjects into two groups, those reading for objective tests, and those reading for the purpose of preparing a summary. In fact, both groups were given both tests. The articles were from *Scientific American*. Multiple-choice questions were compared with essay-type questions as a basis for defining learning purposes.

Figure 1 The smooth, item and search reading tactics which combine to form strategies of reading

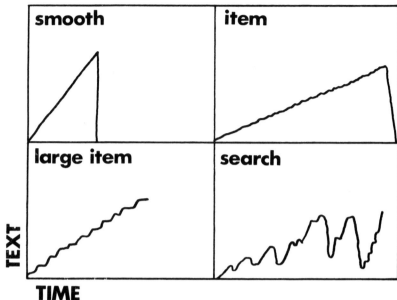

Figure 2 below shows the number of subjects succeeding or failing in an objective and a summary test. A wide variety of materials and purposes were used to establish how the pattern of reading revealed by the machine related to what was learned and to the 'Bloom-type' level of learning it appeared to fit into. Figure 3 (p. 176) shows the reading strategies for those successful in summary and objective tests (A), unsuccessful in summary, successful in objective tests (C), and unsuccessful in summary and objective tests (D). Figure 4 (p. 176) shows that, when tested two weeks later, the loss on objective tests was less for those students who scored high in the summary test.

Figure 2 The number of subjects succeeding or failing in the tests

	Objective tests	Summary tests
A successful in summary tests successful in objective tests	7	19
B successful in summary tests unsuccessful in objective tests	0	0
C unsuccessful in summary tests successful in objective tests	14	6
D unsuccessful in summary tests unsuccessful in objective tests	9	5
Totals	30	30

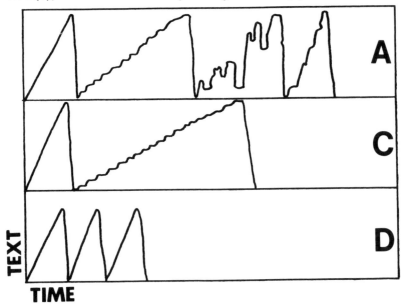

TEXT

TIME

Figure 4 Results of retest after two weeks (60 subjects)

Score on summary	50	47	41	35	31	23	17	13	11	9	6
Loss on objective test	1.8	2.6	3.4	4.0	3.6	7.6	9.3	9.0	10.0	8.2	8.4

It was during this period that the *flow diagram technique* (Johada and Thomas 1966) was explored and developed. It was used first as a way of comparing and contrasting different pieces of reading material. Then we discovered that inking in the details of a person's summary on a detailed flow diagram of the text clearly revealed how selective they were being and the form that this selectivity was taking. It also related closely to the pattern of reading. Hesitations in the record related to what was memorized. (see Figure 5 page 177).

Psychological theories of manual skill had led us to consider the possibility of hierarchical structures of meaning, in which the meanings of words came together to form the meanings of phrases and sentences, the meanings of sentences came together to form the content of the paragraph and paragraphs came together to form sections, chapters and articles. Introspective consideration of these 'levels of meaning' at which one was conscious when reading, reinforced such hierarchical models. We became painfully aware of when we were scanning each word, when the words gelled together into small 'sentence-sized' meaning units and when we were sailing along conscious only of the large chunks of meaning constituting paragraphs or pages.

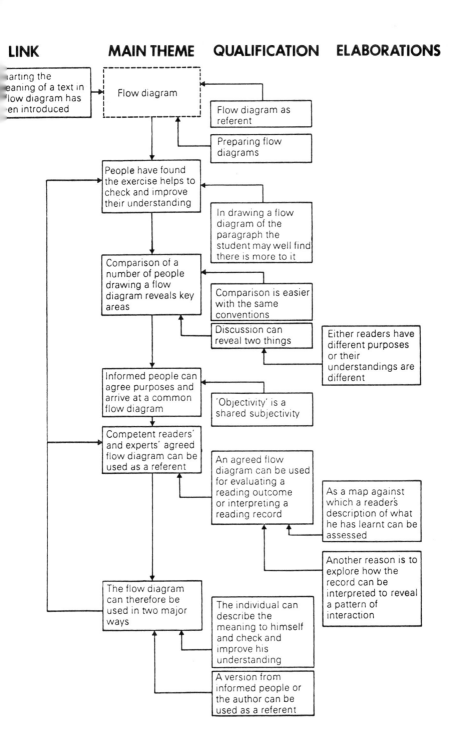

LINK

arting the eaning of a text in low diagram has en introduced

MAIN THEME

Flow diagram

People have found the exercise helps to check and improve their understanding

Comparison of a number of people drawing a flow diagram reveals key areas

Informed people can agree purposes and arrive at a common flow diagram

Competent readers' and experts' agreed flow diagram can be used as a referent

The flow diagram can therefore be used in two major ways

QUALIFICATION

Flow diagram as referent

Preparing flow diagrams

In drawing a flow diagram of the paragraph the student may well find there is more to it

Comparison is easier with the same conventions

Discussion can reveal two things

'Objectivity' is a shared subjectivity

An agreed flow diagram can be used for evaluating a reading outcome or interpreting a reading record

The individual can describe the meaning to himself and check and improve his understanding

A version from informed people or the author can be used as a referent

ELABORATIONS

Either readers have different purposes or their understandings are different

As a map against which a reader's description of what he has learnt can be assessed

Another reason is to explore how the record can be interpreted to reveal a pattern of interaction

Refinements in the development of the reading recorder, coupled with a heightened interest in how complex sentences were read, led us into a consideration of Chomsky's generative grammar and how this related to the meaning structures of our flow diagrams. An exploration of the detailed tactics of word-by-word reading in our sentence experiments convinced us once and for all that reading was a very complex, learned, cognitively controlled, perceptual skill. We were able to show how a person's skill in extracting meanings broke down as we increased the length and syntactic complexity of sentences. By studying the nature of this breakdown we were able to identify some of the psychological mechanisms which were keeping our 'poor learners' from being able to deploy their reading skills effectively.

Finally within this second phase we were able to use our insights into this hierarchically-organized generative process of reading-for-learning (see Figure 6 page 179) to help poor performers to develop their aim insights. They significantly improved their skill in generating from the text just those meanings which they required. In addition to the formal statistical results we were delighted when one technical college teacher wanted to know what we had done to two of his boys. He explained that after three half-day sessions using the machine and flow-diagram techniques they had started to learn and take on interests in learning with a success they never had before achieved.

Putting it to the test: courses in reading-for-learning

At this point in the project our grant from DES expired but we were lucky enough to attract another one from SSRC. Our small success (Thomas and Augstein 1972) in helping people to improve their learning skills led us to feel that we should try to put some of our understandings to the test. We therefore began a series of courses designed to offer students an opportunity to review their skills.

The general approach in all these courses was to use the reading recorder and the flow-diagram technique to enable students to become aware of exactly what they were doing when they were learning. Once they were aware of how they were reading they were encouraged to explore the ways in which this related to the structure of the meanings which they were inventing to fit the words on paper. As they mapped their inventions onto these words they revised and reinvented, mapping onto the words again and again until the degree of matching which they had achieved satisfied their personal criteria of successful learning. (You may find it necessary to explore the sequence of words in the last three sentences more than once before any coherent meaning emerges. Try sticking at it and observing how you go about it. You could even try to divide sentences up into about ten or twelve parts and plot a flow diagram of how each part relates to each other part.)

The first course was at Loughborough College of Education. One of us used the techniques to offer individual opportunities for exploring reading skills. The course followed a well-structured pattern in that we offered

Figure 6 A complex model of the reading/learning process

PERSON READING **TASK INSTRUCTION**

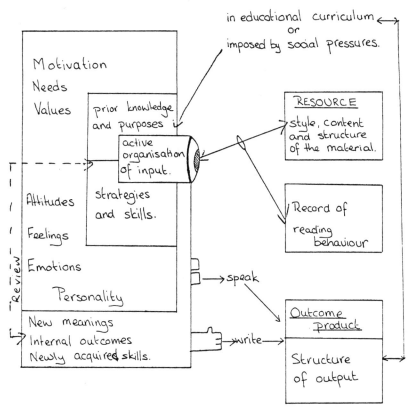

each student the same series of 'modules'. These offered them an opportunity to explore and develop special tactics for achieving high performance combined with rapid reading on each of the learning purposes which were available. Within each module students were free to pursue their own path, but guidance was always available. The results of this course were very gratifying. Students improved on the tasks offered within each module, they improved on a series of 'before and after' tests and their longer-term academic performances made quite startling advances relative to the rest of the students in their year (see Figure 7).

In a course at Gypsy Hill College of Education we used a group-training approach. Students were shown how to use the recorders and how to interpret the reading records. They were also encouraged to use the flow-diagram technique. However, once they had mastered the techniques they were free to explore whatever aspect of their reading skill they chose. In this group the results, as measured against our standards, were more variable, but then so were the student purposes. On measuring success

179

Figure 7 Improvements in educational grades

Gains
Experimental group
+5 0 0 +1 +3 +3 +3 +5 +4

Control group
−3 +3 +2 +2 +1 −1 −2 −4 +2 +1 0 0 0 −1 +2 −1 +1 0 −2 +1 −1 −2
−3

against self-defined purposes 'within-course' improvements were high. Academic performance also improved but not so spectacularly as at Loughborough. This was partly due to a divergence of purposes between students and the more formal assessment procedures of the course.

This problem of institutionally-defined learning purposes and individually-defined learning purposes was highlighted in a third course which we ran for A level students in a technical college. In this case we concentrated our attention on each individual's definition of learning purpose. We used personal interview and Kelly repertory grid techniques. These highlighted the real difficulty in the situation, which was that hardly any of the students wished to be at college, they had little or no interest in getting their A levels and were waiting impatiently to get out into what they called the 'real world'. As we had decided to allow the students to define their own learning-to-read purpose we had to watch most of them decide not to learn to read-for-learning.

This episode proved a rather traumatic experience for the group of young graduates who were involved in running this course. It clearly posed the question of what criteria should be set in developing educational conversational techniques. This question is essentially a moral one: what right has one human being to influence another? When does a teacher say, 'I know you will not like this immediately, but I want you to come along with me for a bit, because in my experience once people have tried this, and got into it a little way, they tend to find that their values change and they get really involved'?

We have run a number of other courses which also demonstrate the effectiveness of this approach to higher-order reading/learning skills. But the dilemma of the encourager of self-organized learning remains. If you encourage someone to be self-organized they may self-organize themselves right out of the field.

New beginnings: developments which have derived directly from these activities

A series of video tapes on learning-to-learn are available from Brunel TV; these include tapes on the reading recorder, the flow-diagram technique and the Kelly repertory grid. They also include discussions on reading problems.

This work has also formed the basis for contributions by all three authors to a postexperience course on reading development offered by the Open University. Contributing to this course was particularly interesting since it confronted us with the need to try to offer these techniques in forms that required no machines and that relied only on the written word. It is our experience that radical challenges to basic skills can be very threatening.

Most people are unaware of how they read. Being faced with one's own record can cause much misgiving. This is particularly true during the stages of a course when students are beginning to experiment with new strategies and tactics. As they let go of their old habits the immediate consequence is that they get worse. They either slow down or learn less well. Unless they are supported through this, the natural tendency is to revert to the old, well-tried, safe methods. A similar process occurs with the flow-diagram technique. At first students tend to reject it as too mechanistic. Then they get involved in it and can become very enthusiastic. Finally they realize that it is mainly a perceptual training device and begin to discard it.

We have not yet properly explored how an organization such as the Open University can substitute effectively for the personal and social support systems which appear to be a necessary cocoon within which new skills can safely emerge. Hopefully a theory of educational conversations may lead us towards some resolution of this problem.

A coherent attempt to apply similar techniques to the learning of mathematics is being made by another member of the Centre, L. R. Chapman, Head of Mathematics, Trent Park College of Education.

Finally David Pendleton is following up work started by one of the authors and students of Loughborough College of Education. They have used these methods with children in both primary and secondary schools. We are currently making a survey of reading strategies and learning performance over an age range of eight to fifteen years. The preliminary results show very little development of higher order reading skills after the age of ten. Most children show very little flexibility in either reading purpose or in the strategies and tactics they bring to the reading-for-learning task.

References

JOHADA, M. and THOMAS, L. F. (1966) The mechanics of learning *New Scientist* 14th April

THOMAS, L. F. and AUGSTEIN, E. S. (1972) An experimental approach to the study of reading as a learning skill *Research in Education 8* November

THOMAS, L. F. and AUGSTEIN, E. S. (1973) *Developing Your Own Reading* Reading Development Unit 7 Milton Keynes: Open University Press

OPEN UNIVERSITY (1973) N. C. Farnes for the Reading Development course team *Reading Purposes, Comprehension and the Use of Context* Units 3 and 4 Milton Keynes: Open University Press

Day 4

22 The right to read

Ruth Love Holliday

Introduction

My paper is based on my experience of two years as Director of a national programme of the United States Office of Education that is focussed on the huge task of eradicating illiteracy in the USA by 1980. We are trying to rescue our eighteen to twenty-five million functional illiterates—the people left behind in the shadow world of noncommunication.

I think the scope of our problem may be more clear to people in Britain today than it might have been a few years ago. Until fairly recently Britain had a homogeneous population holding the same cultural memories, by and large. Change came about slowly, but now the problems—as well as the gifts—of diversity are becoming evident in this country as they did in the USA when our great tide of immigration set in several generations ago. Since we share the same basic culture, we have the same problems—except that our numbers are more overwhelming. And both American and English cultures face the same hazards that militate against holding the attention of the young—the compulsions of television, the enticement of drugs, the faster pace of a technological society, great affluence on the one hand and the pressures of poverty on the other.

I believe that the right to read—the right to literacy—falls into the same category of human rights as those embodied in the first ten amendments to the American Constitution, collectively known as the Bill of Rights. Yet not one of these ten amendments would mean anything to the citizen who can't read them. So the name of the rescue programme I direct is called The Right to Read.

This transcript of a tape that was sent to our office in Washington will poignantly demonstrate my meaning:

> I live in Atchison, Kansas. I was watching TV, and I saw your advertisement on the Right to Read. I know this way of personally sending a tape is unusual, but I felt I could better express my feelings and say more by sending it, so I hope you will accept it.
>
> I have this problem of reading and writing. I have worked for the   Manufacturing Company for twenty years. I quit this job to travel with a Gospel group because it was something I really wanted to do, and now I find I cannot do this.
>
> I was in the National Guard for nine years. I was a drill sergeant.

How I got by I will never know, but I did. No one knows I have this trouble. Not even my family or my wife know my problem. I have been married for twenty-one years, and my wife does not know it.

I can read a little. I read the Bible, although some of the bigger words I do not know, and I read the newspaper. But it isn't enough to do what I want to do. So I saw your ad and thought you could help me.

It is very embarrassing when someone asks you to read and you have to squirm out of it. I have done this, and I don't know whether they suspicion this or not . . . so I hope you can help me.

The Right to Read programme unfortunately has not yet been established in this man's home area, but he was referred to an adult basic education programme in his local school district.

The Kansan said he could read a little, but 'it isn't enough to do what I want to do'. And this is a man in middle life who had managed to earn a living in spite of his handicap. In a sense he was lucky, for in the next few years functional illiterates like this man will not find it easy to make a living. Only 5 per cent of the nation's labour force is needed now for the unskilled jobs of our technological society, and that percentage is decreasing rapidly.

In view of what I have just reported, it seems obvious that we must place the full strength of the American education system behind the effort to teach and encourage reading at every level. We must stop thinking merely of the seven million children in our schools who are having difficulty with learning to read. We must stop dwelling on grade levels and the expectation of failure, and concentrate instead on all the ways in which we can dramatize reading for what it is—the open gate through which everyone starts toward his own goal.

The strain of education

In the past few years education in the United States has been under a continued state of siege. Everyone who ever attended college has felt impelled to voice criticism of 'the system'—and this in a period when more innovation was introduced into schools, more young people entered teaching or teacher training and more Federal funds were allocated to education than ever before in our history. As just one instance of this massive Federal support, the government developed six ways to assist families in financing a college education. As a result, from 1961 to 1971 approximately 60 per cent of those young people who graduated from high school went on to college, although half of them did not complete the four years. And during the 1960s 60 per cent more men and 56 per cent more women graduated from high school than in the preceding decade.

Yet, in spite of the raising of all educational sights during the 1960s, a Survival Literacy Study completed for the National Reading Council in 1970 turned up some startling facts. For instance, one test of reading ability was the ability to comprehend application forms for five such common needs as a personal bank loan or a social security card. Twenty-six per cent of those in the sample who had some college education failed to understand more than 10 per cent of the fifth form, which was an application for Medicaid. There was a 1 to 8 per cent illiteracy range in this group. The illiteracy range among those who had only completed high school was 1 to 12 per cent.

Enter Right to Read

It is hard to explain why a young person capable of entering college cannot read well enough to fill out an application, or why high school graduates can go through ten to twelve years of schooling and leave as functional illiterates. Right to Read is not attempting to explain these things. Rather, it is putting its energies into finding dedicated people to round up and utilize every technique that can make us a nation of readers.

Since, on a national average, three out of every ten American children are reading below their expected levels and capabilities, we believe that there must be multiple causes for this inability. To counter these, we think there should be many-sided approaches and solutions. In developing the 244 Right To Read projects across the country, we first had to research the best programme, those that seemed to be working. After we identified the best methods, we developed reading kits for our centres, each one of which describes a separate programme in a multimedia format.

One kit tells, for instance, how a 'language-experience' approach to reading operates. It explains how teachers are trained in the techniques needed, how youngsters are motivated, how parents are involved, how paraprofessionals are used. It also supplies information about the children who have participated in the tested programme so that there is a basis for comparison with their performance level.

Teamwork is required in setting up and evaluating a Right to Read programme. The classroom teacher is the key person, central to the success of any programme. But she will need the services of reading specialists, psychologists, librarians, and administrators as well as teacher aids and library aids, tutors and student teachers.

The team reading specialist will help the teacher in management, in curriculum development, reading approaches and materials, freeing her to work more directly with individual children and to plan her days.

An idea of the diversity of Right to Read projects, responsive to the demands of a big country, can be realized by a description of some of them. Of the 244 total, 170 are school centres, of which twenty-one are in large cities and have two satellite schools each, and seventy-four are community centres. Each centre is expected to reach 500 persons in a year.

North Star Borough School District in Fairbanks, Alaska, numbers among its 8,600 pupils many Indians and Eskimos whose families move often. Their mobility and consequent lack of reading readiness have created severe problems for both high schools and elementary schools.

Through in-service teacher training to introduce methods and materials which relate to the culture of these pupils, through work with parents of pre-schoolers, and through individualized instruction, the North Star District is helping its students build a sound foundation of reading skills.

The Interstate Research Association, a bilingual research firm in Washington, DC, investigates the needs of Spanish-speaking populations throughout the country with an eye toward a possible television programme on reading readiness for adults.

The National Urban Coalition is developing a pilot project to upgrade the reading skills of welfare mothers. The thirty mothers involved are helping to design the programme, which will aid in basic reading skills. It is hoped that the students can be helped to determine their vocation and reinforce good reading habits in their children. Once the project is set up in one area, it will be studied closely. A resulting report will include recommendations for use of the pilot on a broader scale.

Our philosophy is that Right to Read is for everyone of every age. It is aimed at getting people off welfare, cutting down crime, and making life broader, more productive, and certainly more interesting. Adults teach children, but on the other hand children often get adults into the action.

Diagnosis, motivation, evaluation

The programme descriptions I have mentioned give you an idea of some of the problems Right to Read are trying to meet. But regardless of instructional approach, every programme that works involves first diagnosing the needs of the people involved, and then prescribing techniques to meet those individual needs. Since motivation is so important to the success of all teaching and learning, we try to offer motivational ideas wherever we can and make a collection of new ones as they are observed.

Adults do not need to be motivated when they are pressured by necessity. In the case of children, as I am sure you know, the great thing is to try to find what interests each individual child and to get him involved with learning to read through the incentive of that interest. Failing the development of a real interest, there is always the possibility of structuring a variety of new experiences to ignite a need to know more—the 'more' that can only come through a book.

As for evaluation, we have put a component into each of our kits that should reflect how all the children did on standardized tests but—even more significantly—how their interests have changed, how much time they give to reading once they start getting the 'feel' of it and many other factors that testify to the opening up of new worlds in print. Actually the evaluation components should set guidelines for school personnel so that future programmes can be tailor made to the needs of the students.

Research, technical assistance, staff development

There is no dearth of research into ways of teaching reading. The problem now, as always, is to translate research into usable and attractive methods. Right to Read operates on the assumption that an important part of its mission is to discover what works and why. We have not been in existence long enough to have reached the goals of validation of all our methods, but that will come.

We are constantly looking for new ways to do things, and we try to combine the best we hear or read about from all over the world. In particular, we are heavily indebted to twenty years of English pioneering in open education, for English research and experiment as revealed in the Plowden Report, and for the contribution England has made toward greater flexibility in classrooms and in techniques.

With methods in hand, we ask the school districts we serve to accept our technical assistance. Cadres of Right to Read specialists go around the country to our projects to help assure that the money we are giving to communities is being spent wisely along the lines of planning, operation, and staff development.

Right to Read is particularly interested in seeing that local staffs are developed to put programmes into effect. Each project—as the diversity of our programme examples shows—has different staff needs.

Often schools in the inner city find that youngsters learn more easily and are more comfortable with teacher aides who look and talk like their sisters or mothers than they are with an 'outside' teacher and her air of authority. In any case, in-service staff development can be as innovative as the uniqueness of the setting and situation demands.

Teacher aides, librarians, administrators, and specialists can be developed through on-the-job training and added to the staff as needed. A real effort is being made to obtain released time during the working day for this kind of training at all staff levels.

It has always been my deepest belief that people rather than techniques make the difference. The warm response of a particular teacher is what has traditionally given the initial impetus to some of our best known achievers. Personal involvement and interest give the student more initiative and confidence than any formula we can supply. Thus, because those closest to the problems know best about what is needed, we have asked in each case that the school principal in Right to Read programming be the one to set up a task force of parents, teachers, librarians, and many others to do the programme planning—with our technical assistance as requested. We are not, however, the only ones to offer technical assistance, the school district and the State will be able to aid in many ways.

This local do-it-yourself sort of planning, with leadership from Right to Read, offers the opportunity for general accountability. Responsibility for the success of the programme rests squarely on those who work with it.

Accountability has come to mean different things to different people. To many it means testing and evaluation; to others it means the assessment of performance in meeting objectives. In Right to Read, accountability means responsibility—assuming responsibility for the performance of children, and often of adults.

What about adults?

As I said before, adults do not need further motivation; life has seen to that. If you are embarrassed by your colleagues, put down by your children or the neighbours, that is enough to inspire you to learn how to read more and better. You may be lazy about it until that final moment when some one moment of insight brings you face to face with your inadequacy.

That is what happened to a twenty-seven year old boiler operator in Washington, DC. He was barely able to read and write and had to get his wife to read his bills and personal letters to him. He also had to have help in filling out job applications. But one day when he was signing something on the job, a colleague made fun of him because he wrote his name upside down, as he had all of his life. This, from a fellow worker, was too much, the last straw. He signed up for night classes in adult education.

In reaching out to the adult population of illiterates, we can often start with the children and cure the problems of both children and parents simultaneously.

If Right to Read is to succeed in its goals it will do so by improving education for all. This will be a long haul. Meanwhile, I should like to leave you Right to Read's five basic principles:

1　With the exception of one per cent of the population considered in-educable, people can learn if programmes are designed to meet their specific needs and strengths.
2　Teachers and other educational personnel can adopt new ways if they are provided with methods which they are confident will aid them in working more effectively with their students.
3　Intelligence is native to all ethnic and economic groups, and when expectations are equal productivity will be basically equal as well.
4　The necessary knowledge to solve the reading crisis is available. What remains is for that knowledge to be applied so that it will result in better teacher training, more effective educational programmes, and the use of those new programmes in classrooms and communities.
5　Parents are concerned about their children's educational process and have both the right and the responsibility to be involved in their education.

The contributors

AUGSTEIN, Sheila E.   M.Sc., Ph.D.
Senior Lecturer, Loughborough College of Education,
Hon. Research Member in the Centre for Human Learning,
Brunel University

BEDWELL, Charles H.   F.B.O.A.(H.D.), F.S.M.C., M.I.E.S.
Lecturer in Clinical Ophthalmic Practice,
The City University

CLARK, Margaret M.   M.A., Ed.B., Ph.D., F.B.Ps.S.
Senior Lecturer in Psychology
University of Strathclyde

DALY, Brian   B.Ed.
Teacher
School Psychological Service, Halifax

DOWNING, John   B.A., Ph.D., A.B.Ps.S.
Professor of Education
University of Victoria, British Columbia

FARNES, Nicholas C.   B.Tech.
Lecturer in Educational Technology
The Open University

GILLARD, Charles H.
Head of Science Department
Mill Chase C.S. School

GOODACRE, Elizabeth J.   B.Sc., Ph.D.
Consultant
Centre for the Teaching of Reading, University of Reading

GRUNDIN, Hans U.   Ph.D.
Research Project Director
Department of Educational Research
Teachers College of Linköping

HAYES, Edward   B.Ed.
English Master
Grammar School

HOLLOWAY, Ruth L.   Ph.D.
Director
Right to Read Programme

HUNTER, Elizabeth
Senior Lecturer in Education
Avery Hill College of Education

LATHAM, William   B.Sc., A.B.Ps.S.
Principal Lecturer in Education
Totley-Thornbridge College of Education

McBRIDE, Fergus   M.A., M.Ed.
Lecturer in Education
Moray House College of Education

MacLEOD, Daniel S.
Research Officer
Reading Research Unit
Queen Margaret College

MERRITT, John E.   B.A., A.B.Ps.S.
Professor of Educational Studies
The Open University

MORRIS, Joyce M.   B.A., Ph.D.
Language Arts Consultant

MOYLE, Donald   M.A., L.C.P., L.T.C.I.
Senior Lecturer in Education
Edge Hill College of Education

PLATT, Gerald F.
Senior Remedial Advisory Teacher
Schools Psychological Service, Manchester

PUGH, A. K.   B.A.
Fellow in Reading Efficiency
University of Leeds

RALPH, Phillip H. A.
County Remedial Teacher, Somerset

THACKRAY, Derek V.   B.Sc., M.A., Ph.D.
Head of Education Department
St Pauls College of Education

THOMAS, Laurie F.   B.Sc., Ph.D., F.B.Ps.S.
Reader in Psychology
Director for the Centre for Human Learning, Brunel University

WALKER, Christopher
Senior Lecturer in Education and Reading Tutor
Mather College of Education